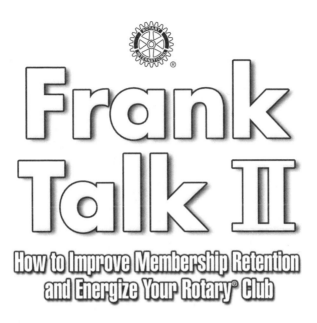

Frank Talk II

How to Improve Membership Retention and Energize Your Rotary® Club

by

Frank J. Devlyn

Rotary International President,
2000-2001

and

David C. Forward

Author, *A Century of Service:
The Story of Rotary Intern*

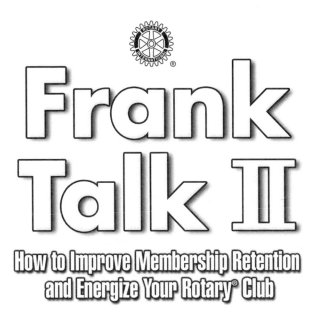

Frank Talk II

How to Improve Membership Retention and Energize Your Rotary® Club

by

Frank J. Devlyn

Rotary International President,
2000-2001

and

David C. Forward

ReachForward Publishing
www.ReachForward.com

FRANK TALK II

How to *Improve* Membership Retention
and *Energize* Your Rotary® Club

For information address:
ReachForward Publishing
14 West Lake Ave.
Medford, NJ 08055-3429 USA
1-856-988-1738

ROTARY®, and are trademarks of Rotary International.
Used with permission.

Printed in the United States of America
Cover photo by B. Aetin Haig. Used with permission.
Cover design and layout: Ad Graphics, Inc., Tulsa, OK

This book is not an official publication of Rotary International.

FRANK TALK II may be purchased individually for $12.95 or at
substantial discounts for bulk orders of 10 or more copies. Rates
are quoted in US funds and do not include shipping and handling.

For more information see the Resource Center at:
www.ReachForward.com
www.FrankDevlyn.org

ISBN: 0-9711030-4-6

This book is dedicated to all those persons who encouraged me to write a book on membership retention. There are too many persons to mention who told me that if we could solve the problem of members coming into Rotary and leaving after a short time, we would have no trouble with membership growth. They made me realize that changes had to occur in this second century of Rotary for it to continue as the premier and prestigious service club it became in its first century of life and service.

I do want to specially mention and dedicate this book to Past Rotary International President Herb Brown. Throughout my years in Rotary he has inspired me with his proactive approach to solving problems in business and Rotary, energetically strengthening both while always being there for the family he loves so much.

—Frank

Within a month of joining Rotary in 1978, another member recruited me to help him on an important community service committee. A few weeks later, another Rotarian personally invited me to attend a multi-district event in which I saw that Rotary extended far beyond my town. Soon thereafter, I was persuaded to attend the district conference—but by then I had become hooked on Rotary!

I dedicate my part of this book to the wonderful Rotarians in the Rotary Club of Marlton, New Jersey, USA (District 7500). They personify Rotary. They welcome veteran and new members alike with true friendship; they work hard to make all Four Avenues of Service come alive through their work. And when pressures of frequent work-related travel caused me to tender my own resignation a few years ago, they refused to accept it, working out an attendance compromise instead. Had those fellow Rotarians not practiced what the pages in this book preach, I would today be one of the lost-member statistics the following pages attempt to avoid.

—David

An Opening Word
from Frank Devlyn

As many in the family of Rotary are aware, my first book called *Frank Talk* openly talked about the benefits and satisfaction of belonging to Rotary. To the surprise of everybody—especially myself—it became a Rotary best-seller. I received many favorable comments that finally somebody had come out with a book that read like a novel and was not simply a report of historical facts and milestones but, rather, a book that told the story of how to overcome the many objections people give about coming into Rotary.

In many of the conversations responding to my story in *Frank Talk*, the comment was made over and over again: "It's great to see you and so many people proactively interested in bringing people into Rotary, *but have you considered that if persons coming into Rotary stayed in Rotary, we would solve all of our membership problems and be ever-growing?*"

Others mentioned that among the many reasons why people who join Rotary soon leave, one is because some clubs have lost their vitality and energy.

I talked with David C. Forward (my famous ghost-writer) and told him, "We have to come out with a book that's going to deal with retention of membership and the reenergizing of a Rotary club."

We decided that I would ask as many persons as possible in the Rotary family to share with us their comments, observations and suggestions on clubs that have been successful in retention and the reenergizing of their Rotary Clubs. We felt that if we could get the stories of these Rotarians and their clubs, these ideas could be shared with the family of Rotary in a new book, *Frank Talk II*.

We also felt that if former Rotarians could tell us why they dropped out, we could show how those obstacles to membership could be avoided in the future. It was also decided that it would be a good idea to use the main characters mentioned in *Frank Talk* to continue their story of coming into Rotary and then, in the course of belonging to a Rotary Club, how they as new members face the problems of retention in their Rotary Clubs.

Because many of my Rotary friends know that I am keen on Internet usage, my webmaster, Rtn. Harriet Schloer, suggested we open a section on my personal website at www.frankdevlyn.org where Rotarians could give us their comments. I also made it a point to end all of my personal Rotary letters with a PS message that they click on their ideas and comments on retention and reenergizing a Rotary Club. In many of my talks to Rotary Clubs I did the same. I wanted the family of Rotary to know that I was requesting ideas on practical, sucessful and innovative ways of keeping Rotarians in Rotary. This new task was much more difficult than getting ideas on how to bring persons into Rotary, the theme of my first *Frank Talk* book which was more successful than I, my close friends

T.D. Griley, Lou Piconi, and even David Forward, ever imagined. As many are aware, David C. Forward, the co-author of *Frank Talk II*, is a highly successful professional writer, much-in-demand speaker, and is the author of Rotary's centennial history book, *A Century of Service*. I am the ideas person, who brings people together to get things done by Creating Awareness and Taking Action, after which I do the promoting. David and I make a good team, and the family of Rotary, starting with me, has to be grateful that David shares his writing talents with Rotary.

I thank everybody who provided their comments on my website, sent letters and emails, and telephoned with their ideas and comments regarding retention and the reenergizing of their Rotary Clubs. A great number of your ideas have been incorporated into *Frank Talk II*.

It is my hope that the many ideas expressed in *Frank Talk II* will help those proactive Rotarians who are looking for ways to improve the retention of their club members and to continuously reenergize themselves.

Muchas Gracias, everybody, for helping make *Frank Talk II* a reality.

—Frank Devlyn

CONTENTS

ABOUT FRANK DEVLYN

Raised on the border between México and the United States, Frank proudly describes himself as bicultural. "As a youngster and student, I spent time in both countries every day," he says. "Home was in Juarez, México, where my mother's family came from, and I went to school in El Paso, Texas. I was immersed equally in both cultures every day of my life."

Frank's father, Frank Devlyn, Sr., a World War I veteran of Irish descent, came from a small town near Chicago, Illinois. Frank, Sr., was an optometrist, as is Frank's mother, Nelva. After they married, they moved to Nelva's northern México hometown of Juarez, the country's largest border city, and opened a small optical shop. Frank grew up in the family business, and worked in the store every day after school. At age nine, he made his first pair of eyeglasses.

When Frank turned 22, his father died. By that time, the Devlyns had opened their seventh optical shop. Frank then had to lead the family business with the help of his mother and two younger brothers. In both hard times and good, the Devlyn chain of optical stores has continued to expand. Today Devlyn Optical Group has more than 500 stores and is the largest retail optical company in Latin America, with branches in México, El Salvador, Honduras, Panama, Guatemala, and the Dominican Republic.

As testament to his prodigious networking ability, Frank sits on the boards of numerous national and international groups. He is frequently asked to serve in a public capacity and it is not uncommon to see Frank being interviewed by the media, Mexican government, or by organizations representing private enterprise seeking his advice.

Frank seems to be hardwired for inquisitiveness. "I like to know how things work, what impact they can have. I'm a constant student, always looking to learn something and apply it to everything else in life. I try to see possibilities and opportunities in everything, failures as well as successes," he says. "Wherever I travel, I look for Rotary successes that can be shared, whether they apply to service projects, club programs or membership development. One of my constant goals as a Rotarian is to take success stories to other clubs."

He joined the three-week old Rotary Club of Anáhuac in Mexico City when he was 29. "I doubt, at that time, whether the larger clubs in town would have invited a businessman of my age." He served as the club's third president. Frank describes joining Rotary as "a turning point in my life," and he brought to Rotary the same energy, determination and forward-thinking that were hallmarks of his business career.

Frank believes that, for Rotary, change is both necessary and inevitable. "To face the new century, Rotary must change. It's the hardest thing in the world to accomplish, but it must be done. Rotary must change with the times, but change with the dignity that our organization requires—while always maintaining those principles that have made our organization great."

His blueprint for Rotary in his 2000-01 presidential year was characteristically ambitious. To help Rotarians accomplish his goals and give meaning and life to the theme of *Create Awareness—Take Action*, Frank appointed 20 task forces. Each one focused on work that Rotary clubs worldwide were doing, he says. Each one had "a specific reason for being," well-defined goals and a plan of action.

"How is Rotary going to adapt to the 21st century? The overriding challenge that we face today is to make Rotary meaningful in the new century, at all levels. Look at the most basic level, club programs. Programs must have the result that members and visitors will say, 'I'm glad I came to that meeting.'" Frank believes that weak programs are symptoms of weak clubs. Programs should be learning experiences and meaningful to new and longtime Rotarians.

Frank and Gloria Rita, his wife of 34 years, have three daughters—Melanie Devlyn-Perez (wife of Juan Carlos Pérez Collado) Stephanie Devlyn-Alcocer (Luis Alcocer Lamm) and Jennifer Devlyn-Maccise (Luis Maccise Uribe)—and six grandchildren: Alexia, Luis, Carlos Francisco, Jennifer, Pablo and Michelle. Gloria Rita has been Frank's partner in Rotary as in life, joining him at Rotary functions at all levels. For that reason, she was made an honorary Rotarian by Frank's Mexico City–Anáhuac Club.

Frank's brother, Jesse, another optometrist, is general director of the Devlyn Optical Group. A member of the Rotary Club of San Rafael, Mexico City, Jesse has served as district governor, committee and task force member, International Assembly discussion leader, and sergeant-at-arms at international assemblies and conventions. Frank has another brother, Pat, general manager of the Devlyn Group, a past president of his Rotary club and a well-known motivational speaker on personal development; a sister, Ethel Devlyn-Gaspar de Alba (Mario) of El Paso; and a half-brother, Gordon, a Rotarian in Elk Grove Village, Illinois. Frank's mother Nelva, a former "woman of the year" of Juarez, was also named an Honorary Rotarian for her civic professional work by the Juarez Integra Rotary Club.

This brief synopsis illustrates Frank Devlyn's commitment to business excellence and community involvement:

- President and chief executive officer of the Devlyn Optical Group of México.

- Past president of the Optometric and Opticians Association of México, the Optical Manufacturers Section of the National Chamber of Industries of México, and of the National Contact Lens Manufacturing Association.

- Attended the University of Texas at El Paso and graduated from the I.P.A.D.E.business school in México.

- Graduate of the School of Optometry of the Mexican Association of Optometrists.

- Regional board member of a leading Mexican bank, Banamex (Citicorp Group).

- Member of the global board of Goodwill Industries International.

- Board Member of Funsalud—One of México's leading health-related foundations.

- Treasurer of the Tuberculosis and Lung Association of México.

- Past Member of the board of directors of the Mexican Red Cross.

- President of México's Vecino Vigilante initiative, a neighborhood watch program sponsored by Rotary clubs, and a broad group of organizations collectively known as "México United Against Crime."

- Board Member of México's "Centro Mexicano Para la Filantropía" which unites México's most reputable philanthropic organizations.

- Past Honorary Board member of The Wheelchair Foundation.

- Past Board member of The Order of Malta/México.

- Founding editor and director of the Rotary regional magazine, Rotarismo en México.

- Governor of District 4170 in 1977-78.

- R.I. director for 1986-88.

- President of Rotary International for 2000-2001.

- Trustee of The Rotary Foundation of R.I. for 1996-98 and 2002-2006.

- Chairman, Avoidable Blindness Task Force, 2001-2003.

- Avoidable Blindness Advisor for R.I.'s Health Concerns Task Force 2003-2004.

- Recipient of The Rotary Foundation's Distinguished Service Award and its Citation for Meritorious Service for his support of its international humanitarian and educational programs.

Frank's first book, *Frank Talk*, told the compelling story of three fictional people he met on a train. When he invited them to join Rotary, they cited common excuses and misconceptions for not doing so, yet he overcame those objections with the result that the three new friends agreed to become Rotarians. *Frank Talk* became the fastest-selling book in Rotary history, with clubs and districts using it as a tool for telling the Rotary story to prospective members. Over three years, more than 80,000 copies were ordered, and the book was translated from the original English into Spanish, Portuguese, Korean, Turkish, and Vietnamese.

As *Frank Talk* was helping Rotarians bring new members into Rotary, Frank was already wondering how he could assist clubs to do a better job of *retaining* their members—and the result is *Frank Talk II*.

About David C. Forwar

David C. Forward was born and educated in England before moving to the United States in 1972. He is CEO of Reach*Forward* Performance Group, and delivers keynote addresses and seminars worldwide on such topics as volunteerism, employee motivation, leadership development, and customer service. He is frequently consulted for his expertise in these areas by the media, including ABC TV and the BBC.

David is a prolific writer, and contributes articles to magazines from Kuwait to Canada. He is Senior Editor of *Airways* magazine, a monthly global review of commercial flight. David's books include:

- *Heroes After Hours*
- *Sales SuperStars*
- *The Essential Guide to the Short-Term Mission Trip*
- *DUH! Lessons in Employee Motivation that Every Business Should Learn*
- *DUH! Lessons in Customer Service that every Business Should Learn*
- *DUH! Lessons in Leadership that every Business Should Learn (in preparation)*

David co-authored *Frank Talk* with R.I. President Frank J. Devlyn, and it became one of the best-selling books in Rotary history, with more than 80,000 books distributed in five languages. In 2004, R.I. released *A Century of Service: the Story of Rotary International*, which David wrote.

He has been a Rotarian since 1978, and has served in many club and district leadership positions. David Forward was awarded the Citation for Meritorious Service for his work as district chairman of the PolioPlus Committee. In addition to his volunteer work in Rotary, David is an elder in his church, and is voluntary president of International Children's Aid Foundation, a ministry that assists orphaned children in Romania.

PREFACE

The following article was written by Barry Thompson, 2003-2004 Membership Development and Retention Chairman. It was first published in the February 2004 issue of *Rotary Down Under* and appears here with the permission of the author and *RDU*.

MEMBERSHIP AND WHY IT'S A PERENNIAL IN ROTARY

by Barry Thompson

"Oh no!" I hear you cry. "Not another diatribe on membership. Haven't we heard it all before?"

Well, have you ever asked yourself why it is that the subject of membership keeps on coming up? Let me suggest that it keeps on coming up because we do not appear to have taken any notice of what was discussed each time the subject surfaced in the past.

A survey by Rotary International recently shows that over the past 11 years the number of Rotarians in Zones 7A and 8 (i.e. Australia, New Zealand and the Pacific islands) has fallen by about 5,800, despite the chartering of new clubs each year.

Indeed if it wasn't for the approximately 4,900 new members who joined those new clubs you can see that we would be in an even bigger mess.

Twenty per cent of our members have been members for three years or less. Twelve per cent have been members for three to five years, 19 per cent for six to 10 years and 49 per cent for more than 10 years.

Twenty-eight per cent of our members are retired from full-time employment, the second highest percentage in the countries survey, and exceeded only marginally by Europe. Women are 11 per cent of our membership against a worldwide average of 13 per cent with the United States of America and Canada (20 per cent), Africa, the Philippines, Korea and Central and South America all having a greater percentage of female members than we do.

Our members are generally somewhat older than the world average with only seven per cent being younger than 40 (world average 11 per cent), with our figures for the age groups 40 to 59 and 60-plus being greater than the world average.

Perhaps even more damaging is that much of our efforts to recruit new members seem to be fruitless in the longer term because we lose more than 40 per cent of our new members before they have been in our clubs for more than three years.

OK, so I've produced a lot of statistics and I know that you can get tired of looking at them, but we do need to look at what these statistics tell us if we are to ensure that our great association will prosper in the future.

To me they say that we are an aging organization having little real success in recruiting and retaining new members and still to recognize that we are in a desperate need of real action to address the membership issue. We need to stop talking about membership and really do something about it.

Why do we need to do so? Aren't we doing lots of service and enjoying ourselves as we are? Of course we are, but to only think that way may soon result in apathy and reduced service.

The world is entitled to demand more of those who say "Service is our product" because there is so much more which needs to be done. We can only meet these demands if we have more enthusiastic Rotarians to share the load and joy of meeting those demands.

In that process we can also do something for ourselves because, as an example, the reduction in membership now means a loss in magazine subscriptions of more than $120,000 each year to *Rotary Down Under.*

More members would mean less need to increase the costs of the magazine. More members should mean reduced District dues and improved support of The Rotary Foundation.

Many of us have experienced life-changing events through the magic of Rotary. Why are we generally so reluctant to encourage others to share those experiences? We were asked to join. That is all it takes to have someone else share our experiences. That is all it takes for us to have more willing Rotarians on whom to call to meet the demands of service.

That is all it takes to reverse the trends revealed in the statistics quoted earlier. That is all it takes for each of us to meet new people who may become our best friends.

That is all it takes for each of us to honour the Rotarian who first invited us into the great fellowship we call Rotary.

Why not share "what's in it for you" with another? You will find that there is even more in it for you.

So what can I do?

I am sure that each of us has been given many ideas on how to address this issue. Here is another, which I know has worked very well for a Sydney club.

A list of classifications was prepared and club members were invited to write names of possible members alongside each classification.

Addresses were added and a circular prepared addressing all the issues that are normally raised when discussing membership.

Five active club members then wrote individual testimonials on their Rotary membership, which were included in a pack distributed to each of the potential members.

The pack also contained information on the club, a copy of The 4-Way Test, Rotary Basics, The Declaration for Rotarians in Business and Professions, and a copy of *Rotary Down Under.*

Two weeks after the mailing, club members followed up the potential members, inviting them to a club meeting where an excellent guest speaker was the attraction for the night. The plan worked and membership in the club has increased.

Will it work for you? *Rotary Down Under* will send a sample of the kits to every club in Australia and New Zealand. All we have to do then is put in a little effort to personalize the documents and send them to prospective new members.

So there is one idea. If you have another successful idea I would love to hear of your success.

Let's not just have words, let's have action.

FOREWORD

by
Glenn E. Estess, Sr.
President, Rotary International, 2004-2005

Retention is one of the most significant membership issues and concerns for our association. Rotary International Presidents have attempted to keep the association's clubs focused and active on retention. They have spoken about the issue of retention, emphasized and supported programs to impact and improve retention. International Assembly training has emphasized the importance of retention to the District Governors and I believe the association's leadership recognizes the importance of and supports the emphases on retention to its clubs and their members.

Members are the basic building blocks and base of our clubs. Without a sustaining and continuing membership base, clubs would only be a group of people meeting on a periodic basis, rather than a group of people supporting a specific mission with a long-term perspective and purpose. A sustaining and continuing membership base allows clubs to develop a core, to develop long-term action-oriented projects, to become vibrant and active organizations initiating change within a community. A sustaining and continuing membership base allows strong friendships and fellowships to develop within a club. With a strong base, the Rotary clubs throughout the world can successfully accomplish the numerous community and international projects and activities they undertake, thus contributing even more to world peace and understanding.

Sustained and stable membership is crucial to the continuing support of Rotary's Foundation through which so much of our service exists. The Rotary Foundation is our Foundation, funded primarily by Rotarians, and its programs are implemented by Rotarians. Increased Rotary membership improves our Foundation programs.

What were the expectations of members when joining? What causes members to become disenchanted with their club? What causes members to terminate membership? What has caused members to terminate membership with your club? These are questions we need to ask and work toward addressing in each of our clubs.

Would an individual terminate membership with a club where they had strong friendships and bonds? Would an individual terminate membership with a club that continually conducted relevant and successful projects and programs? Would an individual terminate membership with a club where they had an involved role in its operations? Would an individual terminate membership with a club that held an esteemed role within a community?

Membership Development and Retention is an ongoing process. It can be a time-consuming and costly process, when not a continuing process. Rotary has developed good and measurable processes for recruitment of new members and extension of Rotary to new communities. We now need to develop equally effective methods to improve retention, and at the same time continue our recruitment and extension efforts.

It is more productive to spend the time, energy and resources to make sure members are connected, involved and happy within a club. Much of our challenge is to establish effective communications with members prior to their considering termination, rather than attempting to determine why they left, after they left.

The association is working very hard at providing clubs with the resources and tools to assist them in their retention efforts, and invites your input with success stories in your club.

On his own initiative, Past President Frank Devlyn has taken the time to present this book to you, which is solely focused on retention. I applaud Past President Frank for his efforts. I hope it will provide you with some thoughtful points and suggestions as to how your club can improve its retention efforts.

INTRODUCTION

"**M**r. Devlyn?"

"Yes."

"Hold the line please. I have a call from the United States for you."

"From whom?" But it was too late. She was making the connection. I waited on the telephone for perhaps 30 seconds, wondering who would be calling. The White House perhaps, with an invitation to dinner? Bill Gates, with an offer to buy my company? It costs nothing to dream!

"Go ahead, please. You are connected."

"Frank!" The woman's voice sounded excited; it was more of a statement than a greeting.

"Yes."

"It's Sue. Sue Keenan, from Rotary. Remember me? We shared a cancelled flight and then talked about Rotary as we rode the train together."

It took me a moment, but then I knew exactly who she was. Almost three years ago, bad weather had caused my flight to be delayed, so to be sure I would make an important speaking engagement on time, I had taken the train. During the journey, I had talked with the three other people in my compartment—Sue, Bob, and Duncan.

I was serving as worldwide president of Rotary International at the time, and as we sped along, getting to know one another, the three of them peppered me with questions about what Rotary was. I remembered inviting them to join their local Rotary club, but each of them had reasons why they disliked that idea. "It's an old boys' club," said Sue. "Rotary club meetings sound *really* boring,"; and, "I can't afford to hobnob with rich people like Rotarians," objected the others. But I explained to them that the *real* Rotary was the Rotary of community service and networking, the great fellowship of friends, the humanitarian presence that helps people in every corner of the globe. And by the time our train arrived, they had all agreed to join Rotary. *That* was the Sue I remembered!

"Susan! Of course, I do. How could I forget you? What a lovely surprise. To what do I owe this pleasure?"

"Well, Frank. You'll remember that after we met, I went ahead and joined the Rotary club in my town. In fact, I sent you a note telling you how our conversation on the train that day had resulted in my becoming a Rotarian."

"Yes, I remember. And I sent you a congratulatory letter, didn't I?"

"You did—you even included a banner with the theme of your year as Rotary International President with it; I still have that, hanging on my office wall. It is the call to action that looks me in the face every day."

"So what's new, Sue?"

"I hate to say this, Frank, but I'm thinking of quitting Rotary. I've been struggling with the decision for quite a long time. My mind tells me to resign, yet my heart urges me to stay. And here's the real problem: I'm president-elect of my club, so if I resign, I'm going to have the guilt of knowing I've left the club in the lurch—that I've let them down. I really need some advice, Frank."

"I'd be happy to help you in any way I can, Sue," I told her, looking up as my secretary slid a note across my desk. But the problem is, I'm flying to Argentina in a couple of hours, and I've just been told that my car is waiting to take me to the airport."

I heard a sigh on the other end of the telephone. "Oh, Frank! I'm sorry. But I should have made it clear; the reason I suddenly thought of calling you in Mexico City is that our district governor visited my club yesterday, and she said that you were coming to speak at our district conference. *That's* where I was hoping we could talk."

I looked at my watch. I still had a couple of minutes to spare. "When is your conference?" I asked.

"April 25th to the 27th," she replied.

I quickly flipped through my planner. There it was. The president of Rotary International obviously cannot attend all 528 annual district conferences in more than 160 countries around the world. So he appoints senior leaders, generally past presidents and current or past directors, to represent him at many of the conferences. By coincidence, it seemed he had assigned me to be president's representative to the very district where Sue's Rotary club was located.

"Well, what do you know? I have it right here. I'd be delighted to sit and chat with you, Sue."

She seemed at once pleased—and relieved. "Oh, and Frank...?"

"Yes?"

"Do you remember Bob?"

"Of course. The computer dude!"

"That's right. You know, he and I joined the same Rotary club. But he also felt disillusioned, and he hasn't been to many meetings lately. If I can persuade him to come, may I bring him, too?"

My secretary was now gesticulating urgently.

"Of course you may. Why don't you round up Duncan and we can have a reunion—just the four of us."

"Okay," she said. "Duncan joined the evening club in the next town, so I'll try to contact him, too."

"All right. Look, I arrive on Thursday, April 24th. My time during the actual district conference is pretty much taken up by official activities. But why don't we get together for dinner that Thursday evening, since my flight gets in at two o'clock and I have no other commitments that night. Say, seven o'clock at the hotel's restaurant?"

"That's *perfect*," said Sue. "I'll take care of getting a reservation and inviting Bob and Duncan. Oh, Frank, thank you *so* much. I'm really looking forward to seeing you again."

"I am too. And now, I really have to get to the airport," I told her. "See you in a month. Thanks for calling, Sue."

I hurried down to the waiting car, where my bag was already waiting. As we drove through Mexico City's clogged streets, my mind wandered back and forth between nervousness about whether the traffic would ease so we could make my flight, and the call from Sue. The problem she identified was real. For years, Rotary had emphasized membership growth—yet had devoted scant attention to membership *retention.*

During my long flight to Buenos Aires, I thought about the times many of us had launched membership campaigns. Awards were given, clubs and districts with extraordinary recruitment achievements were publicly applauded—all the attention was on bringing *new* members into Rotary.

And then what?

In some parts of the world, districts that had won the contest with double-digit percentages in membership growth then had a double-digit *decrease* in membership the very next year. Some membership growth has occurred naturally in recent years. The rule change that permitted women to become Rotarians led to tens of thousands of new members since the late 1980s. Then the emerging democracies of formerly-communist countries saw the formation of hundreds of Rotary clubs in once "closed" nations—and thousands of entrepreneurs and leaders who wanted to join Rotary's global network.

I remembered a priest telling me that he counsels couples who go to him to be married with the advice: "It is quite easy to find someone who will agree to marry you, but it takes real hard work, constant communication, and total commitment to *stay* married." Was it any different with Rotary clubs?

The old rule of thumb was that 10 percent of members leave Rotary every year for "natural causes." They die, retire, move away, lose their jobs, etcetera. So if every five years half the members of any service club leave due to attrition, that club needs a 50 percent increase every five years *just to stay even.* But within that club, existing members are aging, some of them are getting tired of being called on to do the same jobs year after year. The other side of the argument is that the same people *do* perform the same jobs year after year, so new members quickly lose their enthusiasm because they feel their talents and energy are not needed. So the problem is that many clubs need to energize their programs so they can retain more of their members—especially their new ones.

I looked at the in-flight map. We were over the Andes. Far below, I could see snow glistening off the jagged peaks in the moonlit night. As I reclined my seat to take a nap, I thought back to that foggy day when I had met Sue, Bob, and

Duncan on the train. Each of them had freely shared their misconceived ideas about Rotary, and yet three hours later, the four strangers had become friends. It had thrilled me to hear them all consider joining Rotary. And yet, I must admit, I was a little skeptical. "It is an easy promise to make when you know you'll never see each other again," I recall thinking.

But they *had* joined Rotary. All three of them. And now, less than three years later, at least two of the trio are thinking of leaving. I thought to myself, "It took a lot of courage for Sue to call me." It would have been much easier for her to simply drop out, to fade away—as Bob had apparently done. Sue must really care about Rotary to have taken the time, trouble, and expense to call me in México.

Suddenly, membership retention was no longer a committee title or seminar topic; it had become a personal mission.

CHAPTER 1

Getting Reacquainted

"Frank! You haven't changed a bit. How are you?"

It was one month and five days since Sue had called me at my office, and now, as I walked up to the maitre d's station at *Ristorante Enzio*, it was her voice that greeted me.

"Sue!" I said, turning to my right to track down the source of the greeting. The maitre d' escorted me to the table where Bob and Duncan were seated. Sue was already heading toward me, and in an instant we were all exchanging handshakes and hugs.

For several minutes we each learned what had happened in one another's lives since we had met that day on the train. Duncan was enjoying his retirement immensely. "When I visit friends still in the company where I spent my entire career, I feel like they are in a different world from the one I so enjoyed," he told us. "Taking that early retirement package was the smartest decision I ever made in business. It is just not the same there any more, there's so much more pressure. People are being forced to do more—with fewer resources." But he protested at my description of him being a man of leisure.

"Leisure!" he exclaimed, "I'm busier now than I ever was before." He had enlisted in several volunteer organizations, still traveled extensively, and proudly told us he had taken up golf and scuba diving.

Sue told us that her business, which provides consulting services to travel agents, had gone through a rough time. "All the airlines suddenly stopped paying travel agent commissions," she explained. "That was their major source of income, so thousands of agencies went out of business, or merged with larger agencies." Bob asked her how travel agents could even survive today when their airline commissions have disappeared. "They charge fees for the services they provide—and of course, they do still earn commissions from tour and cruise operators. Actually, I was able to turn lemons into lemonade. It has been a great opportunity for my company to show my clients how they can make the changes not only to survive, but to prosper, in this new business environment."

"You know what?" Bob interjected. "I don't even *think* of travel agents as bricks-and-mortar businesses. Whenever I book a trip, I do everything online. I booked my entire honeymoon over the Internet—the flights, the hotel, the cruise—everything."

"Honeymoon!" I exclaimed. "I didn't know you have gotten married."

"Yes," Bob affirmed, with just a hint of a smile. "Sarah decided it was time to make an honest man of me, so we tied the knot in February—on Valentine's Day, actually."

"That is so romantic," said Sue, her head slightly tilted, as if she were watching a movie.

I suddenly realized that we had been sitting together for several minutes, chatting away, and that Duncan had hardly said a word. "So what's been going on in your life, *Amigo?*" I enquired.

"Well, Frank, life is good!" he declared. "You know, it took me quite a while to do anything about Rotary after our meeting on the train that day. Then I was on a trip to Australia, and the jet lag really hit me hard. I couldn't sleep past about 3 a.m., so finally, at about six o'clock; I went downstairs, intending to take a walk. But it began pouring with rain, and as I hung around in the lobby, picking up some sightseeing brochures, I noticed a sign on the wall that showed the local Rotary club met in that very hotel on that very day for breakfast. So I decided to drop in.

"It was quite an experience. Even though I told them I was not a Rotarian, they welcomed me as if I were a long-time friend. I told them how I'd met you on the train, and the guy I sat next to invited me out on his boat for a day of fishing. Apparently, someone in the club sent my name through to the club in my hometown, because about a month after I got back, they called and invited me to attend a meeting. I joined the club about five weeks later and have really enjoyed being a Rotarian ever since.

"Oh, and let me add my own congratulations on your marriage, Bob," Duncan added. "Did you two ever join Rotary?" He gestured at Bob and Sue.

Bob looked down at his place mat and began playing with the knife, twirling it around. "Yeh, I joined," he replied, without a glimmer of enthusiasm. I noticed that the smile had also disappeared from the normally effervescent Sue.

"You sure don't seem very excited about it," observed Duncan. "I've seen people more enthusiastic about funerals."

Sue managed a nervous little grin. As usual, she spoke first.

"Bob and I are in the same club," she explained. "We haven't really spoken to one another about this before we came here; it's not as if we've compared notes. But I think both of us are feeling a little let down. Bob, why don't you share what's on your mind, and then I'll bring up my issues."

But before he could speak, the waitress appeared at our table. We suddenly realized we had all been so involved in conversation that none of us had even looked at the menu. While the server went to fill our drink orders, we examined the menus, and by the time she returned, we were able to tell her what we wanted for dinner. It was a good ten minutes before we were able to resume our discussion about Rotary.

"Okay, Bob. What's the problem?" I asked.

He seemed reluctant to talk, but gradually he opened up. "The truth is, Frank, I'm bored to tears at most of my Rotary club meetings. First of all, most of the people there are at least twice my age. Secondly, I feel like an outsider. There are several cliques in the club; I actually went to sit at a seat one day—the only open chair in the room—and was told, 'That's reserved. We've always had the same eight guys sit together for 20 years.' I had to have the restaurant set up a new table and sit at it by myself until some members arrived late and joined me."

"Hmm. I bet I know the clique you are talking about," Sue chirped in.

"But even the meetings...they're so...booorrring." He pronounced the word as if it had an extra two syllables.

"In what way?" I enquired.

"Singing, for starters," he volunteered. "Frank, I'm 34 years old. I live life in the fast lane. I drive a Porsche. I run the I.T. department where the average age is 27. Then I dash out to a Rotary meeting where a bunch of 70-year-olds delight in singing *Wait 'till the sun shines, Nellie.* A couple of months ago, I took a couple of friends whom I thought I had sold on the idea of joining Rotary. They're both about my age; one's a banker, the other a stockbroker. When the club started singing these songs from our grandfather's era, I thought my guests' eyes were going to pop out of their heads. *I don't sing,* Frank. And if I did, for darned sure I wouldn't let rip in public with renditions from the Greatest Hits of 1925."

"Well, I can..."

"I'm not finished," he interjected. "I don't want to burst your bubble or be offensive. But you asked me to be honest about my feelings toward Rotary, and that's what I'm being. Let's talk about programs. Half the time—okay, perhaps that's an exaggeration—one out of every three weeks, I would show up for Rotary and discover there was no program that day. You don't realize; the work environment is different from the way it was when all those old retired guys were in business."

"Hey, watch it! I'm an old retired guy, remember?" Duncan interrupted.

Bob laughed out loud and touched Duncan's shoulder reassuringly. "I will *never* think of you as an old guy." Duncan smiled appreciatively.

"But seriously," Bob continued. "You just cannot imagine the pressure of the modern workplace. We don't get two-hour lunches like they did in the past. I don't even *get* lunch most of the time. They've laid off 20 percent of the people in my department and business is up 26 percent—so we're under incredible pressure to do more work with fewer resources.

"Then, on the one day of the week when I sneak out of work and dash off to the Rotary club for lunch, I feel like an outsider. I don't have fun, there's almost nobody close to my age or with my interests, and often times, no speaker. I don't need to pay dues for *that*." He almost spat out the last word.

"I'm sorry," Bob added, looking around the table. "I didn't mean to dump on you all. I know you are all Rotarians now, and I *know* Rotary does wonderful work, but my experience just hasn't been very positive. You asked me about my life in Rotary, and now you probably wish you had never brought it up."

"That's not true," I replied. "Look, although we only met once before, I feel as if we are friends. And friendships can only grow if each person is totally honest with one another. But before I address some of the issues you brought up, Bob, I'd like to ask the other two about their experiences in Rotary, okay?"

He nodded his agreement.

"Duncan, how long have you been a Rotarian, now?"

"Eleven months."

"And how would you describe that experience?"

"Well, I *love* my club," he began. "Of course, my circumstances are different. I don't have the pressures of work any longer—thank goodness. And my club meets in the evening, so it has a more relaxed atmosphere than some breakfast and lunch clubs I have attended. However, we *always* have a program. I cannot tell you how much I've learned from the speakers we've had at Rotary. Last week, the mayor spoke to us on the new park the city is planning. There have been times when I arrived and saw the topic of that night's speaker and thought, 'Oh, how dull is *this* going to be?' But then they give a presentation that's informative and interesting. I don't think I could count five times when our program has not left me feeling more educated or entertained.

"And in our club, we're not *allowed* to sit in—what did you call them?...cliques. When we arrive at the meeting, each table is numbered. There are ten seats to a table, and so as you arrive, you put your hand into a covered box and pull out your number. That signifies the table at which you then sit. So every week, I fellowship with different members. It's been great.

"I think, to be honest, that the average age in our club is a little higher than 31," he added. "But age is never an issue. We are *one* club. I'm as happy to chat with the new 25-year-old we just took in as with a septuagenarian. And I honestly believe every member feels the same way. You should see us when we work on a fund-raising campaign or a community service project, I could just as easily be teamed up with the retirement-age bank president as with the young teacher who joined recently."

As I listened to Duncan, I wondered how two clubs in the same organization—two clubs in neighboring communities—could be so different in their attitudes and culture. I turned to Sue. "That's the longest period of silence I've witnessed since I've known you. Where do you fall along this continuum?" I asked. I recalled the telephone call from here a few weeks ago when she had revealed her own frustrations with her Rotary club—the same one to which Bob belonged. I wondered if she would simply repeat his observations, or could there be yet *more* problems?

"Well, I don't know quite how to put this," she began. "I'm normally such a positive-thinking person. I can find the silver lining in every cloud. So I feel rather embarrassed now to think negatively. But to tell you the truth, I...I..." As I looked at Sue, I could see her eyes glistening. I realized that whatever was on her mind was quite an emotional burden. "I'm thinking of quitting Rotary."

"*Great!*" I thought to myself. Two out of the three superb Rotarians I introduced to Rotary are leaving—less than three years after they joined. That's a 66 percent loss ratio. If my business only retained 33 percent of our customers, we would go bankrupt. My mind snapped back to the conversation.

"Sue, let's just talk. What is it that makes you feel so frustrated?" I asked.

She took a deep breath and began. "First of all, it's the money. Some of the movers and shakers in our club kept complaining about the food at our weekly luncheons. They convinced the board that we would not be able to recruit top-class business leaders if we met at a family restaurant, and they pushed through a vote that moved our meetings to a hotel that's considered the best in town. It *is* a lovely place—very elegant—but our meal prices have increased by 40 percent. When I told the board that this might scare away some of our members who live on fixed incomes, they told me, 'Those old-timers have more money than you and me put together.' Another board member said, 'This is a professional organization. The prestige of our new meeting place alone will make people want to join.' Frankly, it's not just the old people I am worried about—it's me, too! I have a small consulting business. I'm just getting it started. They can say, 'The company pays people's dues.' Well, guess what? I *am* the company! And I believe the purpose of Rotary is to serve, the purpose of Rotary is not for it to be a gourmet dining club."

Sue took a sip of her Merlot and continued. "A few weeks after I joined the club, the secretary was transferred. Nobody else wanted the job, so the president asked if I would take it. I wanted to help, and thought it would teach me a lot about Rotary—which it did. So I agreed. Back on July 1st, our new board of directors took office, and a couple of months later, the president-elect had a heart attack. He was replaced by the then-vice president. But about a month later, her company transferred her to London. So the board asked if I would step in and become president elect."

"That's *wonderful* news, Sue," said Duncan. "You see, they recognized true talent when they saw it."

"Oh, you're such a sweetheart," she said, smiling at him. "But you see, *that's* the problem. I've taken courses in leadership before, when I was in the airline industry. I only agreed to be president elect because I thought that by the time I became president, I would be able to lead the club to new heights. I don't *need* this job. I don't want it for *me.* I thought I could be a president who could really make a difference."

"And why don't you still believe you can?" I asked.

"Because they don't want a leader, they want a *caretaker*," she replied. "I've tried everything to motivate them. I've suggested new fund-raising ideas. I've proposed a membership development plan to bring in new blood. I realized that the same four people had served as the Four Avenues of Service directors for *eight consecutive years*—so I nominated a slate of different officers, people who could bring fresh ideas to the club. And do you know what the response was?"

It was a rhetorical question to which I don't believe she expected an answer. But Duncan interrupted her with one anyway: "They vetoed your ideas," he proffered.

"Yes! They have said, in one form or another, 'We don't *want* new ideas. We see new projects as work. We like things the way they are.' Bob is right; they *are* a bunch of bores. They either never had the same Rotary ideals you sold us on, Frank, or they have long ago lost sight of them.

"So, as Bob said, I've begun to think, 'Why am I wasting my time on this? Why am I spending my hard-earned money to go through these frustrations?' But I feel guilty, because as mad as those stick-in-the-muds make me, there *are* some good people in the club. And the other reason is, I made a commitment. So if I quit, am I letting down the nice people? Am I letting Rotary down? As I see it, there are three options: stay and give in; stay and do it my way; or quit. What do you think I should do, guys?"

I realized that three sets of eyes had turned on me. I thought of my speech I had written for the district conference keynote the next night. Of how I had labored over exactly the right message that would at once inform and inspire the hundreds of Rotarians and guests at the opening banquet. But *this* was an infinitely more difficult assignment. These were real-world Rotarians with real-world problems, and they were looking to me not for motivational platitudes, but for real-world solutions.

Rotary *needed* the likes of Sue and Bob, and the conversation we were about to have would likely determine whether it kept them—or lost them forever.

CHAPTER 2

The Big Tent

"**W**ell, let me start by telling you how glad I am that you called me," I said to my fellow diners, still wondering what my next words would be. "It took a lot of courage for you both to open up as you did; it would have been a much easier route for you to just drop out of Rotary and fade away. But I believe with all my heart that if you were to do that, both you as individuals and Rotary as an organization would lose. And who knows what child would not be reached, what needy person in your community, or important contact somewhere in the world would also never be reached?

"But I don't want to get philosophical. I want to be as open and honest with you as you have been with me. Let's take a look at the big picture for a moment. Rotary has more than 1.2 million members. Are all of them motivated, cause-driven visionaries? Of course not! Look at any large organization—a religious denomination, a political party, a trade union, a huge company. You will find a small number of jerks, and a lot of drones who lack vision but can be counted on to at least show up and get the work done. But in any 1.2 million-member organization, you will only find a

small percentage that will emerge as true leaders—
and the masses will sometimes rebel against their
ideas because they are addicted to the status quo.
Some people, whether they are church members
or Rotarians, hate change, and anybody who pro-
poses new ideas can feel as if they are on a futile
mission. But you need to see the larger picture.
That corporation, that church, *that Rotary,* is far,
far greater than those individuals—or even the local branch that is causing so much anxiety. We
are all under the big tent of Rotary—but we are
not all motivated by the same things.

"Now, Bob, listen to me carefully, because I
don't want you to mistake what I am going to say.
You and I could very easily cast aspersions on those
people who always sit together. Frankly, I think
it's ridiculous for them to do so—and outrageous
for them to tell you not to sit at their table. That is
certainly *not* the Rotary fellowship I've witnessed
over the past 34 years.

"However, Stephen J. Covey, in his book *The 7
Habits of Highly Effective People,* says we should
'Seek first to understand before we seek to be understood.' So let's try to do that for a moment. What
if these old men are genuinely best friends? What if
they have been that way for longer than you have
been alive? What if they feel a little insecure about
even how to communicate with your generation?
Their identity was based on values and experiences
such as military service, personal relationships, age
barriers that were more rigid, frugal financial management—things that many of them believe are
simply unacceptable to Generation X. They might

have never once even touched a computer. Now, imagine how they would feel at having to maintain a conversation with folks of your age and with your interests.

"I am going to say it again: I am not *condoning* their actions; I am just trying to explore a possible *explanation* for them. Again, go to any synagogue, church, or mosque, and you will find some people who always go to the *same* seats and worship with the *same* friends and then go out to lunch to the same restaurant afterwards—and they've followed that pattern for years, maybe even decades.

"Let me accept your definition of that group as a clique, for the moment. We could have two schools of thought here. The first theory could be that one person's clique is another person's circle of friends: *So what? What's wrong with wanting to eat lunch, or play golf, or do other things together once a week?*

"The other theory holds that cliques don't belong in a fellowship organization such as Rotary. So let's not focus on the problem, let's focus on the solution. Just as I suggested that *you* try first to understand before trying to be understood, so should the other members of your club. Especially those people who comprise the clique you mentioned. What if somebody were to explain to them the consequences of their actions? I'll bet they have no desire to offend anyone, and have no idea that they have already done so. Perhaps it should be one of their friends, perhaps the club service director or the president—maybe the issue could be raised at a club assembly without having to confront specific individuals. Just remember that old axiom I learned for dealing with unacceptable employee behavior: *Hate the sin, love the sinner.* Your goal should be not to lecture them or label them as bad Rotarians, but rather to illustrate to them the *consequences* of their acts and attitudes."

Bob had taken out his Palm Pilot and was jotting down some notes. Our dinner had arrived several minutes ago and mine was getting cold. "Duncan," I said, "I don't have the franchise on brilliant ideas. You mentioned how your club avoids cliques. Tell us more."

And so he did. He explained that friends often arrived and sat together for a drink at the bar before (or after) the Rotary meetings. But at the meeting itself, they reach into a closed box and retrieve a number—and that is the table at which they then sit. Thus it is mathematically inconceivable that the same ten friends could draw the same table number week after week. "The only exception," he added, "is when someone brings a guest. In that case, the secretary finds another tag with the same table number as their host."

"Let me be a contrarian for a moment," I interjected. "Bob, you've pretty much dropped out of Rotary because you feel no connectivity with the other members, right?"

He was still punching notes into his PDA, and let out a barely discernible affirming "Uh huh."

"And Sue, one of *your* goals is to energize the club so that the members will accomplish more during your upcoming presidential year."

"Right."

"So let's think about this for a moment. The number one reason people *join* a service club civic group or religious organization is because friends invite them to do so. Friendship—or fellowship, as we call it in Rotary—is an incredibly powerful force. Can we all agree on that?" I looked around the table at three nodding heads.

"Then doesn't it follow that one way to increase one's enjoyment of a Rotary club is to create more bonds of friendship within the club?" Again they nodded. "So if you could find more people who shared your interests, you'd likely enjoy going to Rotary more, right, Bob?"

"Of course."

"Okay, I'll avoid pointing out that if nine other 30-year-olds who were nuts about computers and fast cars were to become Rotarians—and good friends—that *some* members of your club might call you a clique..."

"Hmm, *touché*," Bob grinned.

"My question is, how can you make more people feel more connected to the fellowship of a Rotary club?"

"Frank, may I say something?" asked Duncan.

"Of course!" I said.

"When I was in Australia, I visited a Rotary club in Brisbane. They had started a program they called 'Club in a Club'. The concept was essentially to form small groups that had specific shared interests based on age, hobbies, vocations—whatever. It was so successful that they expanded it to other clubs in their district. The guy told me it was common to add ten or 20 members at a time— all in one 'Club in a Club'—and he said membership retention was far better than with traditional recruitment programs."

"That's a *great* idea," said Sue. "Do you know how I can learn more about it?"

Duncan pulled out his notebook. "Let me see..." he said, flipping halfway back through the book. "I may be retired, but I'm still an engineer at heart. I make notes on everything. Here it is! They have a website with the entire plan laid out for you to follow: www.geocities.com/club_within_a_club/index.html."

Duncan's report of the Australian idea reminded me of the International Fellowship Groups that already exist within Rotary. Rotarians from around the world who share common interests— attorneys, golfers, dentists, music-lovers, skiers, persons interested in eye care, persons fighting AIDS—communicate with one another to share their dual bonds of service to humankind and their particular avocation. But this idea brought that concept down to the local club level. I tried to imagine how a club with a dozen Duncans—retired, community-minded professionals with lots of available time—could do for a community. Or a group of Sues or Bobs, with unlimited enthusiasm and the drive to make a difference in the world.

"Remember," I told the trio. "For as much emphasis as we have in Rotary on serving at the community, vocational, and international levels, everything starts with club service. It is not just the responsibility of the club president or board of directors—it is *every member's* duty to ensure that it is a fun, fulfilling, enriching experience to attend their weekly meetings. That means it is our personal responsibility to avoid making another member feel excluded. But it also means we should individually and collectively be proactive about creating new opportunities for fellowship with one another."

"I'm beginning to feel a little guilty," said Bob. "I realize that I cut and ran from Rotary for the wrong reason. I was thinking about myself, while the whole point in joining Rotary is to think about others. Maybe I lost sight of the important things and made too much of the clique thing."

CHAPTER 3

Not My Cup
of Tea

"But..."

"Oh no! Not the dreaded *But!*" It was Sue, of course, reacting to Bob's hesitant addition.

"I can understand your points regarding cliques. But remember what I told you: *I hate that singing which my club insists on doing.* Every darned week it's *I've been working on the railroad,* and *Wait 'till the sun shines, Nellie.* You know what? I've only ever *been* on a train once, and sure as heck I'm not interested in *singing* about working on the railroad. Dude, this practice is *so* 1920s. I'm mortified at having to stand and sing these old songs—even though I actually only lip-sync them. Those friends whom I took to the club meeting as prospective members to this day still kid me about the singing."

"How do the other members of your club feel about singing?" I asked.

"Oh, I suppose many of them *do* love it," he replied, rolling his eyes.

"The majority of them?" I enquired. "Do they sing because that's a tradition they're going along with? Or are they about as enthusiastic about singing as you are opposed to it?"

Sue answered for him. "I think the majority of our members really enjoy it," she said. "Personally, I don't have a problem with it, and although I empathize with Bob, I think it would be enormously controversial if we tried to stop singing. I mean, Bob, we only sing two or three songs. What does that represent, five minutes out of a 90-minute meeting once a week?"

"Sue, I'm not saying the club is wrong, or the Rotarians are *bad* for singing. I'm just saying it is so *not me*. What was it Frank said a while ago? 'Hate the sin, love the sinner.' I don't hate the Rotarians, but...well, how's this for a dreadful pun: I hate the *sin-gin'*, not the *sin-gers*." Bob smiled proudly at his word play; the rest of us groaned loudly.

"When I conduct sales training workshops, I teach my clients that to be effective salespeople, the first thing they need to do is empathize with the customer. So, Bob, *I hear what you are saying*. Then I tell them to *isolate* the objections. Bob, tell me again what your issues are with our club?" Sue took a notepad from her briefcase and removed a pen from her jacket. She was in full sales training mode!

"You said that you hated the singing. You felt like there were cliques. The cost of the meeting was an issue. What else?"

"Uh...the lack of organized programs and speakers," said Bob. "Oh, and the age thing."

"Yes, don't forget that. The club is full of old has-beens like me," chortled Duncan with theatrical disgust.

"Man, how many times do I have to tell you not to take that personally," Bob objected, defensively. "I'd love it if there were 50 guys like you in my club. You prove the point that age is a state of mind, and in *my* mind, you are certainly not old."

"Boys, boys," cautioned Sue, waving her finger at them. "So let's look at these objections you've identified: singing, cliques, lack of speakers, average age of members, and cost. Now considering everything, let's rank these in order of importance to you. Which do you consider the most important problem?"

Bob carefully considered his answer before speaking. "I guess my biggest objection is the lack of programs. I feel my time—especially during the work day—is extremely valuable. When we have meetings at work, we make every minute count. I don't believe in fluff. If we're going to take the time to gather a group of professional people together, we need to make that time productive for all concerned. I joined Rotary to make a difference, to give back, to network. And when I show up for a meeting and the only thing that happens is that I eat lunch with a bunch of people with whom I have little in common, I feel frustrated and let down."

"And what's the next highest on your list?" Sue asked.

"I suppose it *was* the cliques. But I feel a lot better about that issue now."

"Okay, so shall we cross that off the list?"

"Sure."

"And the next-highest ranked objection?"

"I don't know, Sue. I've never thought about quantifying my thoughts before. Let me look at your list." She slid her notepad across the table to him. He studied it for at least a minute before speaking again.

"You see," he began. "The cost is only an issue because I don't feel I am getting much out of the meetings. If I were, I don't think I would mind the cost. Same thing with this." I looked over and saw him pointing at Sue's notation *"Average age."* "Like I said to Duncan, I don't hate a person's age, just when they exclude me *because* of their age, and then sit around complaining, refusing to help with club projects because of an attitude that they have paid their dues in years past."

"I understand. So that leaves the singing," she summarized.

"Yes."

"So what you are saying is that singing is the objection to Rotary which you rank lowest?"

"I guess so."

"Boy," I thought, "she's good. I wonder if she would come down to México and do some sales training for my staff." But Sue apparently was not finished.

"Bob, let's now play 'What if?' Go with me for a moment on this. Let's pretend you are a member of a Rotary club where you really felt welcomed, where your fellow Rotarians included you in their fellowship. It is *fun* to go to Rotary and associate with them. Can you picture this?"

"Okay."

"And every week you just *know* there will be a good program, and interesting speaker, and you are sure you will come away feeling more fulfilled than when you walked in."

"So far, so good."

"You love being a Rotarian. You don't even have enough fingers and toes to count the number of friends you have in your club. And it's an active Rotary club; you help out in community service projects, you and Sarah even volunteer for an international humanitarian trip."

"You have just described how I feel about my club," said Duncan.

"Me, too," I volunteered.

"Now, Bob, you can picture yourself in that situation, right?" Sue continued.

"Yes," he replied.

"How does it feel?"

"Great! That's the Rotary to which I wanted to belong."

"Okay. Now, let me add one thing: the club members sing a couple of songs at their meetings each week. Would you quit the club?"

"Sue! I *trusted* you! You think you've got me, don't you?" He was laughing as he pointed a finger accusingly at her.

She sat upright in her chair, assuming the posture and demeanor of a judge. "The witness is ordered to answer the question," she said, the corners of her mouth revealing a little smile. "Would you leave your perfect Rotary club just because they continued to sing?"

"Of course I wouldn't," he admitted.

"And why not?" Sue asked, her voice now soft and inquisitive.

"Because the perceived *benefits* of membership to me would far outweigh the minor personal annoyance that I felt about the singing," he said.

I was impressed. Duncan caught my eye and he silently communicated that he was, too. But the battle had not been won yet, as we realized when Bob spoke again.

"But Sue, I'm not *in* the Perfectville Rotary Club. Frank may have persuaded me to look at the clique problem from a different perspective, but the other issues—the lack of programs, the cost, the generation gap—they are real. They exist in our club. You are right, I probably could live with the singing, but I can't live with the whole package. From my experience so far, Rotary is just not my cup of tea."

Sue put both hands on the table, her fingers spread apart; she leaned forward noticeably. "Bob, that's why I need you. Our club isn't even close to meeting its potential. If we were a car, we'd be firing on two cylinders. The reason we're all here tonight is that I was so disillusioned with some of the same elements you are complaining about that I was ready to resign. But now I realize that would be the wrong thing to do. Wrong for me—I am not a quitter. How would my clients feel if they saw me run away when the going got tough? It would be wrong for Rotary, too—we are committed to serving humankind, and I now realize that I can accomplish much more as a part of a service club than I can do by myself. And finally, it would be wrong for me to let down the members of our club whom I like, and who entrusted me to be the next president.

"Remember what I said earlier? That I believe I have three options: to stay in the club and give in to those who want the status quo—and have a year in which our club essentially stagnates even further. Or option two, to stay in the club but to use every ounce of charm, persuasion, and leadership I can muster to have a year of service initiatives and progress. Or third, to quit Rotary. What do you think I should do, Bob?"

"Sue, I think you have all the right motives—and you certainly have vision and leadership ability. I think you should stay and do it your way."

She almost pounced on him. "Then do it *with* me, Bob! We both have similar ideas for using our talents in voluntary service. We both can see beyond the obstacles to the possibilities. You see a table of boring old stick-in-the-muds, but I say, look at Terri and Jim; look at Phil Warner and Janet Mason. Look at...oh, what's the name of the new member...the vice president of Commerce Bank?"

"Pat O'Donnell."

"That's it. These are people who are like us. They *want* to be active; they've got lots of ideas. They want to belong to a *service* club, not a luncheon club. If we leave, we let *them* down, and how long will it be before they lose interest and quit? Why don't you join my leadership team and see what we can do together?"

"Okay, Sue. Maybe I should. Where would you like me to serve?"

"How do you feel about international service? I feel we should broaden the horizons of our club so that members can better appreciate the global nature of Rotary's outreach. I was even hoping we could host a Group Study Exchange team next year—and perhaps adopt an international service project."

"I would love to," Bob affirmed. "Where can I learn more about that sort of thing?"

"Permission to speak?" I interrupted. They all laughed. "You already have your answer, right at this district conference. I'm looking at the conference schedule the governor sent me, and tomorrow afternoon, there's a presentation by the district GSE [Group Study Exchange] committee chair, and

I see that on Saturday morning there is a workshop called 'International Service Ideas.'"

Bob asked me to repeat the details as he punched at his Palm Pilot again. "Got it!" he said, with noticeable enthusiasm. "I'll be there."

"Well," said Duncan. "I believe this calls for a little celebration. Anybody want to join me in a quick rendition of *I've Been Working on the Railroad?*"

Bob faked a punch at him, barely making contact with Duncan's arm.

"Ouch!" he complained. "Don't hit an old man."

"You deserved it."

"Yes, I suppose this time I did. Now can we discuss something serious, such as what we should order for dessert?"

CHAPTER 4

Booorring!

I t bothered me to hear Bob describe his attendance at Rotary meetings as boring—or, as he put it, "Booorring!" Yet I knew, deep down in my conscience, that he was not only speaking the truth—he was not the first person to voice this complaint. It certainly would not be a fair indictment to label all—or even *most*—Rotary clubs with this epithet. But his was not the *only* one to be defined thus.

Marriages fail, relationships end, employers lose good workers all for the same complaint Bob aired—people get bored. In my year as Rotary International President, we had launched a global campaign to bring new members into the organization. By every measure, the effort was successful. But I had also seen recent reports that many of those clubs that had won awards for membership development had not done so well at membership *retention*.

As Rotary's long-term members age and die, we need the vitality of these new Rotarians to maintain and grow our clubs and service activities. When I became aware of the membership retention problem a few months ago, I started asking around for ideas. "First, why do people leave, and second, what are some of the most successful membership retention clubs doing to prevent it?" I wanted to know.

To my surprise, several people (whose opinions I respect) came back to me with variations on Bob's complaint that they found Rotary meetings boring.

Harold, a friend and past district governor (PDG) himself, complained that the worst offenders are often PDGs, who "read mostly long, boring speeches...over and over" at club and district functions. "I once had a District Conference program from the 1940s and noticed that the program was almost identical to the one I was attending 50 years later," he reported, adding, "You have to look at it from [the new or prospective Rotarian's] viewpoint. Not [those] who have committed to Rotary for so many years that they overlook its deficiencies...We are not motivating 85-90 percent of the members...we need to create new energy and frankly address the situation."

Harold's words had haunted me for a long time. Was he being overly critical? Perhaps. But as I reflected on the dozens of district conferences to which I was sent as the RI President's representative or as an invited guest speaker every year, I noticed—after Harold's comments made me think about the problem—that a great number of key presentations were assigned to PDGs, and other speakers, who gave some truly boring reports. Admittedly, Bob had complained about being bored at his club meetings, whereas Harold's criticism was mainly leveled at dull district events. But many of those PDGs make the circuit speaking to clubs, and certainly one of any incumbent governor's objectives is to increase attendance by rank-and-file Rotarians at district events. So either way, it is a problem.

Bob Menconi, another friend (and a past R.I. Director) wrote me: "Truthfully, if I was invited to join many of the clubs in my own district, I would run [away] as fast as I could." In a comment that could have been directly tied to the problems Sue and Bob described, Menconi had added, "Why are some clubs more successful than others? Maybe in the way they are structured and motivated. Rotary International has nothing to do with the structure, it is the will of the people." He said that if the local club is boring, find out why it is so, then "tune it up...maybe you should change the format..."

If we are to indeed get to the root of the problem, then perhaps we should follow Harold's advice and not leave membership development and retention to 'old men with gray hair' (i.e. most PDGs. As they say in the American South, *Them's fightin' words* to some. But on reflection—and I only even consider this stereotype to make the point—how successful can we be at communicating the excitement, relevance, and personal rewards of Rotary to 30-year-olds if we are a 65-year-old whose glory days were as a district governor 20 years ago? As I had developed this thought, I had also wondered how I could communicate it effectively. How could I make the point that I was not criticizing everyone who was a past district governor? How could I avoid the impression that we only want 30-year-olds to join Rotary?

Certainly the ClubinaClub concept should attract more people with shared interests, and that alone should help make meetings more interesting. Another suggestion I had heard from several people was to reduce the time often spent on announcements and club business. You can only hold a member's attention for so many reports before they begin voting with their feet.

Perhaps we should experiment with different meeting formats—especially at district events, which typically have attracted a declining percentage of Rotarians—and few new members—in recent years. I wondered what *this* district conference would be like if people like Bob and Sue were given the freedom to run it with the proverbial clean sheet of paper.

I remembered that some time back in México another Rotarian, PDG Freddy (Federico) Compean, told me he equated Rotary with a store, and our club leaders as the store's salespeople. Many clubs "tend to spoil the merchandise by letting their meetings become boring or tedious, which prevents the club (the store) from bringing in new members (customers)," he said, adding: "I am convinced we *must* make our meetings pleasant, interesting, and fun. Would you sell as much if your stores did not pay attention to its customers?"

Another old friend, Cliff Dochterman, who was president of Rotary International in 1992-1993 once pointed out that the Rotary club meeting must compete with all other activities in the life of a member—family, vocation, television, hobbies, community, church, and their children's school and extracurricular interests. "So the weekly meeting must be so worthwhile that it can compete favorably for a Rotarian's time, money, and commitment," he concluded.

I had thought of Rotary clubs as being in competition for a member's attention before, but if I combined Cliff and Federico's metaphors, I came to a frightening realization: I thought of the many large, famous, formerly-successful department stores that were once the retails anchors of cities across America—almost all of which were now out of business. And why had this happened? Because they continued to do business the way they had always conducted it, while not realizing that the tastes of their customers had changed. Could the same thing happen to some Rotary clubs? It took me only seconds to think of several Rotary clubs that once had hundreds of members—they were among the largest and most prestigious in the world—and whose membership is today fifty or seventy-five percent less.

With clubs like Bob's, which continued to function the way they had operated for more than a half-century, could the same fate befall many Rotary clubs? I feared that unless they eliminated the boredom factor and created an atmosphere where attending the club meeting was more appealing than other temptations at work or home, then some Rotary clubs could be on the same downward-spiraling path as such once-proud stores as Philadelphia's John Wanamaker, Bullock's, Gimbel's, Jordan Marsh; B. Altman's in New York; Woodward & Lothrop in Washington; Baer and Fuller in St. Louis; G.C. Murphy, Montgomery Ward, and W. T. Grant.

So what should a club do so its members would never label it with the epithet "boring"? I thought back to the thousands of Rotary clubs, district and international events, and conversations I had had with other Rotarians over the years. Which programs, ideas, and examples had stuck out as examples of best practices?

I looked around the table at the three Rotarians chatting away to one another. They were cracking jokes, swapping stories, and Duncan was asking Sue for travel advice about South Africa. I realized that this contented trio—or foursome, if I included myself—was a microcosm of a Rotary club. A *good* Rotary club. Here was a travel agency consultant, a retired engineer, a young computer guru, and a Mexican optical chain owner. Which reminded me, I had been wanting advice on buying a new laptop computer—who better could I ask than Bob? So the first requirement was to bring together people of diverse interests so that they could exchange advice and ideas.

The second requirement is to bring together folks who really enjoy one another's company.

And third, *having fun* is the one sure-fire antidote to the problem of boring meetings. Leah Ewing Shaw, a Rotarian in Florida, once told me, "If *location, location, location* is the motto of the real estate business, then *laughter, laughter, laughter* should be the motto for my club...Who in their right mind would quit this club and miss out on all the fun?"

The very word "fun" is so simple, yet so difficult to define in the Rotary context. It does not mean we sit around telling jokes, or pulling childish pranks on one another. But think of your very dearest friends; remember how enjoyable it is when you get together? You *really* have fun. Now it would be hard to define what that "fun" is in that analogy, but you will know it when you experience it.

From the earliest days of Rotary, the most successful clubs have made sure that members had fun at the meetings. Indeed, although the fact may disgust Bob 100 years later, it was Harry Ruggles, the fifth member to join the original Rotary Club of Chicago, who sprang to his feet during an unusually dull moment in the club's meeting and said, "Come on, fellas, let's sing!" Bob may feel the tradition is dated for his generation today, but many clubs have unquestionably used singing to increase the sense of fun and fellowship over the past century. My emphasis is not on the singing, but on the fun that the Rotarians have *during* the singing. If the majority of the club members consider singing to be a fun activity, the practice in that club should continue.

As I ruminated on the topic, I realized that I kept using two words synonymously, *fun* and *fellowship*. The dictionary does not consider them to have exactly the same meaning, and they are not necessarily synonyms in Rotary either. Yet they are not mutually exclusive. Taken individually, they are each solutions to boring meetings. But in Rotary, we take the concept of fellowship to a whole new level.

Fellowship means the camaraderie of meeting with other business and professional leaders who share the commitment to serve humankind. We have fun when we fellowship with those Rotary comrades, and fellowship stems from those with whom we have fun.

But in Rotary, the word takes on a larger, more global definition when we refer to Fellowship Groups. John Eberhard, a Rotary International Director from London, Ontario, Canada told me, "Fellowship is the glue which attracts and sustains the Rotary experience." He called the Rotary experience "a wonderful intercultural smorgasbord of new friends and insights—an amazing network of service through fellowship [and] friends around the world."

What *are* fellowship groups? They are—to borrow a phrase from the Brisbane Rotarians—clubs within the larger Rotary clubs, centered on Rotarians' vocational or recreational interests. Imagine an attorney who happens to be a Rotarian: she could join a fellowship group of other attorneys from all over the world. My friend, past district governor Fred Otto, chairs the lawyer's fellowship that communicates, meets, and even exchanges home visits, to expand their global professional network while learning more about how the law is applied and practiced in different countries.

Virtually every conceivable hobby is covered by a fellowship group. So Rotarians who enjoy sailing, stamp collecting, fishing, cooking, golfing, and bicycling (among many other activities) get together for special trips, meetings, and adventures at which they share their passion for their hobby—and all of them also share the common bond of being Rotarians.

I know private pilots, who belong to the International Fellowship of Flying Rotarians, who have used their own airplanes to fly humanitarian relief supplies into areas struck by natural disasters. Other friends belong to a Rotary dentists' fellowship and they organize mission team trips—and yet others who participate in the barbershop quartet fellowship group provide some of the entertainment at international conventions.

These recreational and vocational fellowships have existed for many years, but there was a growing desire on the part of Rotarians to serve through special interest groups—especially those that are health-related. Now we have them. The Rotary International Board of Directors approved the Rotary Eyecare Fellowship, the Fellowship for Repaired Hearts and many others that afford the opportunity for fellowship and humanitarian service in a member's specific area of interest. For example, what was originally a Rotary World Community Service project became Heartbeat International, and that program now supports 50 centers around the world—all sponsored by Rotarians—where the needy are given pacemakers free of charge. Let's say you are a Rotarian and have a special passion for children with heart problems; through this special interest group you could be a cardiologist who volunteers your time and expertise, or a non-medical person who decides to hold a golf outing to raise money for the program.

What's my point? The point is that when we provide an outlet for people to do what they enjoy doing; they are much more likely to stay and contribute, rather than let give up and quit. John Eberhard from London, whom I quoted a moment ago, told me, "I have been playing in my club bridge [fellowship] for 33 years. No member of my fellowship group has left Rotary. So it proves to me that friendship is an important factor in membership retention. My canoeing fellowship does annual river cleanups. That kind of active involvement [and service to the environment] nourishes the friendships and makes Rotarians connect with one another. At the weekly meetings, they bask in the stories and memories of the fellowship event. The reasons for membership come full circle."

Cliff Dochterman, without knowing of John's comments, validated those points when he told me, "Seldom do I see a Rotarian who is an active member of the Fellowship of Golfing Rotarians, or Fellowship of Musicians, Yachting, Computer Users, Scouting, Recreational Vehicles, or dozens of other special interest groups, ever withdraw from Rotary."

I smiled as I focused on that term in Cliff's final sentence: *Special interest groups.* It is a term used pejoratively by political opponents during election campaigns, as in, "He has sold out to special interest groups." In that context, nobody would admit to being a member of a special interest group. But we could make a case that in Rotary, the key to membership retention is to create and encourage opportunities for our members to participate in special interest groups.

We are all members of Rotary—but sometimes that fact alone is not enough to make us feel "special." Yet when I hook up Bob with a group of computer wizards, and Sue with Rotarians who are business consultants, and Duncan with an international fellowship group that is passionate about travel—now we have linked their Rotary membership with topics in which they have great personal interest.

Finally, even the word "group" is relevant. Our business world has become more high-tech, yet as human beings, we need to be more high-touch. We spend hours each day staring at computer screens, communicating by e-mail, instant messaging—even video conferencing. Even the way we shop has become depersonalized. The very incident that created that spark in Paul Harris' mind to begin the first Rotary club was when he saw how shopkeepers in a Chicago neighborhood greeted a lawyer friend of his so warmly. Today, much of our shopping is done over the telephone—or via an even-more impersonal channel, the Internet. Our shopping habits have changed, in less than a decade, from face-to-face to technology interface. All the more reason, therefore, for Rotary to provide a brief respite from this impersonal world, where people can leave their computer screens and cell phones and, for a brief period each week, get back to the invaluable, essential, and irreplaceable opportunity for fun and fellowship with a group of professional friends. That meeting, as a group during a Rotary gathering, is the lubricant the human spirit needs to keep going. Forget to add it, and the soul seizes up.

My mind was suddenly drawn back into the conversation at the table. I gathered that Bob had brought up the subject of the frequent lack of speakers at his club meetings, to which Sue suggested that *he* fill in the next time there was no program. "Are you crazy?" he was saying. "I'd rather walk on hot coals than speak in public. I'm terrified about having to address a group; when I have to run a meeting at work, I break into a cold sweat."

"All I'm saying, Bob, is that you shouldn't complain about the problem unless you have an idea for the solution," Sue chided. Then turning to me, she explained, "I was telling him, the woman we had as our club program chair has been very sick. She's been in and out of the hospital for about nine months, so we have had no consistency with anyone booking the weekly speakers for the best part of a year. Sometimes we have one—usually when they call the club asking if they can address us—but usually we do not."

"Bob," I said. "What sort of programs do *you* think would make for interesting club meetings?"

He did not hesitate before answering. "First of all, any program other than *no* program," he began. "You know, Frank, I can't give you a magic answer, firstly, because I don't have one, and secondly, because we need 52 programs a year, so *diversity* should be the key word." I thought he had finished, but apparently he was still processing his answer.

"We had settlement on our new house a couple of weeks ago, and I put the mortgage through Commerce Bank. Pat O'Donnell from Commerce had just joined our Rotary club and so I put the loan through her. Because I had never had a mortgage before, I asked her a lot of questions at Rotary one day, and at her suggestion, we met for lunch shortly a couple of days later. I asked her how she liked the club, and guess what? She said she was frustrated because she had attended something like eight meetings and there had only been two or three guest speakers. Of course, she deals with lots of interesting and influential people in town, and before lunch was over, we had made what we think would be the right way to plan the programs for the entire year. She said something to the club president the next week and was essentially just brushed off."

Sue looked flabbergasted. "Why don't you tell *us* what you two came up with," she suggested.

"Well it all begins with the need, we believe, to plan things well in advance. For example, Rotary has four Avenues of Service: Community Service, International Service, Club Service, and...uh..." He searched his mind for the final one.

"Vocational Service," I added, stifling a smile as I recalled how many times I had heard it described as the "Forgotten Avenue of Service."

"That's it, Vocational Service," Bob affirmed. "So first of all, we discussed breaking each year into four. We would look for speakers who could present topics that fall into one of those avenues—roughly—once every four weeks. Let's take International Service, for example, since that's the area that first attracted me to Rotary. We should jot down all the interesting programs and focus areas that fall under International Service. I can't remember what we came up with now, but for starters, let's say we have PolioPlus, International Youth Exchange, that peace program The Rotary Foundation just started, oh, and Frank's pet project that provides cataract surgery in developing countries. You get the idea. Now, we look at a calendar and since we want roughly one out of every four weeks to be about International Service, we go to the district, or other clubs that have experts in PolioPlus and we ask for a speaker for week one. Then we get a speaker for International Youth Exchange for week four, and the peace scholarships for week eight. Meanwhile, we fill in the blanks for the intervening weeks for the other avenues of service.

"We would look at the calendar and when we see dates that have significance, for example, United Nations Day, we would arrange programs that are relevant to the occasion. Pat was great. She said she has a client that is a TV station and she suggested arranging a behind-the-scenes tour for the club one evening, while they were broadcasting the news. That made me think about one of our club's members...who's the old guy with *The County Times?* The one with the toupee?"

"Bud."

"Yes, Bud. We talked about asking him to host a field trip as a program to learn how a newspaper is produced. She asked him the next week and he agreed immediately. I just think that anything that helps us understand how other businesses oper-ate is really interesting. And isn't that what Vocational Service is all about?"

"It certainly is," I said.

"Bob, do you think Pat would be interested in serving as program chair beginning July 1st?" Sue asked. "That's just a few weeks from now, and she could start booking the programs right away."

"We could ask her," he replied. "I sensed that she was quite interested in helping in that area. She certainly has the contacts."

"Sue," I added. "I do believe you are beginning to learn Leadership 101: find good people and give them ownership of the work they like to do. It seems to me as if you are beginning to assemble a first-class team for your presidential year. There is an old adage in Rotary that suggests 'The only time you can say *No* in Rotary is the day they ask you to join.' From what I have seen and heard, you, Bob, and this woman Pat have vision, leadership skills, initiative, and ideas. If I give club presidents one piece of advice it is this: 'Don't try to do every-thing yourself. Get others who think like you and put them on your team.' You mentioned other names of people who don't have that old stick-in-the-mud attitude that so upset you. I think it's time to take them out for coffee to uncover *their* vision and sense for where they can contribute to the club, too.

"I learned something from the first Rotary club meeting I ever attended. Forty years ago, my brother Jesse and I were in Sulphur Springs, Texas, visiting one of our company's major suppliers, and the principal took us to his Rotary club as his guests. We noticed some aspects of Rotary that still ring true: the friendliness of everyone in the club and the fact that the members were all outstanding representatives of their vocations. The program was about insurance fraud and how it was investigated. I didn't know anything about Rotary at the time, but I remember saying to myself, 'I learned something today.' Even today, one of the great strengths of a good Rotary club is programs that inform, educate, inspire, and entertain."

I shared with them some of the other thoughts about fun and fellowship that had come to my mind earlier. By the time *our* coffee arrived, these two frustrated, almost-*former* Rotarians were motivated and exchanging ideas with Duncan and me about how to energize their club, recruit new members, expand the fellowship activities, and commit to new service opportunities.

They had moved from being part of the problem to being part of the solution—and best of all, they had come up with most of that solution themselves.

CHAPTER 5

Unmet Expectations

"**F**rank? Frank Devlyn? Is that you?"

I turned almost 180 degrees to see who was calling me. From the rather dimly-lit area beside the maitre d's station I saw a tall, thin man with a completely bald head, his shiny scalp reflecting the light from the ceiling above. I had no idea who he was. But having been seen by tens of thousands of Rotarians around the world during my many speaking engagements, I realized that many people had seen *me* whereas I had no idea who *they* were. The man waved off the maitre d' and walked over to our table. I rose to greet him.

"Hugh," he said, reaching out his hand. "Hugh MacRae. Remember me? We met at the International Convention in San Antonio the year you were R.I. President. You autographed your book for me."

"Of course! How have you been? What are *you* doing here?"

"I'm the District-Governor Elect, Frank. Just six weeks to go before my year begins. Say, Frank, I was thrilled when the governor announced you were to be the R.I. President's representative here, and I was going to ask you for some advice. Do you have a couple of minutes?"

"Actually, Hugh, I'm just finishing dinner with three of the best Rotarians from your district. We're trying to come up with some good membership retention ideas; you are welcome to join us for coffee or a drink."

Everybody stood and shook Hugh's hand as they made their introductions. Bob reached over to an adjacent empty table and pulled up a chair, and each of us moved a little closer together to make room for our new guest. Sue was the only one who recognized Hugh, having attended a President-Elect's Training Seminar [PETS] for incoming club presidents throughout the district. But neither she nor Hugh had ever talked one-on-one.

"So, it's membership retention that's on your mind, is it?" asked Hugh, in a heavy Scottish accent. "Do you know that very subject is very close to my heart?" It was a rhetorical question. Before anybody had an opportunity to respond, Hugh resumed talking. "Y'know, Frank, I mean no disrespect by this, but for years various past district governors and past-R.I. presidents have gone on and on about membership growth. I believe it was an ego thing for some of them: they wanted to show that huge increases occurred in new Rotarians during their watch. But a year later, they're out of office, the trophy the club president received is gathering dust somewhere, and his successor watches as members who were recruited in a giant numbers contest leave the club in droves."

"Why do you think those new members leave?" I asked.

"Broken promises," he answered, without hesitation. "Actually, two reasons. The first is the broken promises—unmet expectations; the second is the lousy way in which they were introduced to the club."

"Unmet expectations? Broken promises? What do you mean by that?" I asked, a little nervous about whether his frankly-voiced opinions would sting a little.

"Let me give you an example," he said. We get a new Rotary International president, and come hell or high water, he's going to go down in the record book for having the highest increase in membership in history. At the International Assembly, where every district governor in the world who will serve in his year goes to be trained, this president motivates and inspires them and delivers the thinly-veiled threat that unless *your* district has double-digit membership growth next year, you will not be helping the team; you will not be considered a very effective governor. He holds up crystal statues emblazoned with gold stars and tells the assembled governors-nominee they can either be stars—and win this award—or meander around aimlessly at ground level. Each incoming hears that every district in the world will have their new-member statistics published for all to see in *The Rotarian* each month, and they feel a stirring inside their hearts: *We want to win that award. We want to shoot for the stars!*

"Now, the first set of expectations is already being set up to be broken. You see, three or four years ago, none of those folks embarked on a journey to be governor just to win some tacky plaque from an R.I. president who had not even been nominated for his position then. At some point over the next year, most of those governors will feel let down by their clubs, and will not win any star awards. Their year will end on a bittersweet note; some clubs will have resented their constant messages of 'produce numbers, produce numbers.' Worse yet, the governor who replaces them will bear the brunt of the decline in membership resulting from so many of those new members who quit, because they were not recruited properly and soon find they have their own set of unmet expectations.

"And what motivated those people to join Rotary during the big membership campaign? Well, just as the R.I. president inspired his governors, so the governors motivated their club presidents with workshops and speeches and newsletter articles on 'sure-fire methods of attracting new blood' and 'Every club's new-member statistics will be printed in the governor's newsletter each month'. Who wants to be at the bottom of an achievement list? Not any governor, nor any club president. So the club presidents make membership growth a central theme, they form competing teams within the club, and put up a bar chart every week that depicts who is winning and who is losing in the membership-growth contest.

"So now I'm a grass-roots member of that club. I want to do my fair share. I enjoy Rotary. I believe in it; I like this year's president and want to help her have a good year. And I am an entrepreneur. That means I tend to respond to challenges. So I go on a recruiting campaign.

"'Hey,' I say to my chiropractor, 'You're just opening your own practice. Wanna join Rotary?' And when the car salesman and chiropractor ask what is in it for them, I make allusions to the business potential in the club, pointing out that Rotarians prefer trading with other Rotarians. And when the funeral director and pastor express doubts about the weekly attendance requirements, I tell them that we do not strictly enforce those any more. When the young insurance agent asks what Rotary is, I expound on its boundless networking possibilities. And when the Realtor expresses a concern about the cost of membership, I use that line our district membership chairman gave us: 'You've got to eat lunch *somewhere*, haven't you?'"

"So they always have one objection less than I have an answer to overcome it, and they join the club. A few months later, the honeymoon is over. The people who joined for the sales opportunities haven't sold anything to the other members—in fact, they sensed hostility at even being solicited. The networkers got nowhere. Instead, they felt like they were intruders, that many members were insular—almost like cliques."

I looked at Bob and he was already shooting knowing glances at Sue.

Hugh continued: "The people who joined because they really did want to make a difference in their community felt let down—not a single volunteer opportunity was given to them in their first six months of membership. And the folks who joined despite their concerns that the dues would strain their budget were hit with a double blow: some of the club members complained about the food, and the new restaurant they moved to caused a 25 percent dues increase. As if that was not enough, there were constant additional solicitations: $150 for a club Valentine's Day dinner-dance, a strong-arm pitch for a $1,000 contribution to The Rotary Foundation, and a special fund-raising campaign for this and that special cause."

I saw more looks exchanged between Sue, Duncan, and Bob.

"So a few months after their triumphant entry into the club, they begin to drift away. Why? Because *their* expectations were left unmet. And in the worst cases, Rotary membership was oversold and the promises were under-delivered—and they left with a negative impression of Rotary."

"Wow! You sure don't hold back on your opinions, do you?" Sue commented, when Hugh had finished speaking. "I find that refreshing. I have only been a Rotarian for three years, but I feel I can bear witness to some of the attitudes and incidents you just outlined."

"Look...it's Sue, right?"

"Yes."

"Look, Sue, first of all, I don't want you all to think I am negative about Rotary. Far from it. And also, the scenarios I just described were a composite; I'm not suggesting they would all happen in one club or at one time. I was being overly dramatic to make a point. Ethical conduct in all we think, say, and do is a central tenet of what we Rotarians believe in. But sometimes, we need to be more brutally honest with *ourselves*. We need to recognize that our own egos, or pursuit of numbers for numbers' sake, drive our decisions. And whenever we act that way, we—and our clubs—will pay the consequences."

"Hugh," I asked. "What is your solution, then?"

He raised his index finger to make a point. "Firstly, do not misunderstand me. I am *not* against membership growth. I'm the first to say that we need more members and should all do our part to bring new blood into Rotary. What I *am* saying is we need to take a marketing approach rather than a sales approach."

"What's the difference?" Duncan asked.

"I've already described the sales approach," Hugh answered. "It is the single-minded drive for numbers. But the first rule of marketing is: find what the customer needs, then provide for that need. So the marketing approach begins with an honest evaluation of the club today. What are its strengths, what are its weaknesses? Don't fool yourselves! What defines *your* club? Characterize its membership, its programs, its activities, and the true cost of membership. Even ask an outsider—without 'selling' him on Rotary first—to attend a few meetings as your guest. Then ask him or her to

quantitatively evaluate several of his or her observations of the club—say, using a five-point scale.
How friendly were the members toward the
stranger? How would he describe them? When he
enquired of them what Rotary—and this club—was
all about, how did they respond? How favorably did
the meeting location, time of day, program activities, service projects, etcetera, reflect on Rotary's
mission? If he were to be invited to join this club,
would he do so? Why, or why not? Would he be
enthusiastic or cautious about doing that?"

"Hugh, it's getting late," said Duncan, glanc-
ing at his watch. "I don't want to be rude, but I
thought you were going to talk about membership
retention. It sounds to me as if you are describing
membership *recruitment.*"

"Actually, you are right—and wrong," the
Scotsman continued. "My point was that you need
to know who you are and who your targeted members are—how your strengths and weaknesses
mesh with his or her desires and dislikes—before
you start trying to recruit members. After this in-
trospection, you have the opportunity to fix things
that need to be corrected in order that the club is
more attractive to prospective members. For example, if you do not have good, interesting weekly
speakers, or if you find that there is a strong con-
sensus for helping kids—get those in place before
you look beyond your current membership.

"Now let me fast-forward, because you are
right; it is getting late. Assume you've got new
members, you've found the right candidates—what
comes next?"

"You get a bill?" Bob replied. We all looked askance at his comment. "That's what happened to me!" he protested. "The day they inducted me into the club, the secretary said he couldn't give me a Rotary pin because he's misplaced them. Then the treasurer handed me a bill and told me dues are payable by the 10th of the month, and since this was something like the 12th of that month, could I mail him a check."

Sue and Duncan shook their heads in disbelief.

"I have always maintained that a well-informed Rotarian makes for a better, more loyal Rotarian," I said. "There is a big difference between being a member of a Rotary club and being a Rotarian. I think Hugh is right: it is very important to find and fix any root causes of problems within the club, and to know what makes membership a compelling proposition. I believe the most important step to having long-term, quality members starts on the day they join the club.

"In fact, I need to correct myself. It begins *before* they join the club. There should be an orientation committee that meets with each prospective new member, after he or she has attended a few meetings. If possible, I even suggest the prospective member's spouse, partner, or family be present and the orientation committee should give a straightforward appraisal of the club's culture, attendance requirements, financial obligations— and opportunities and rewards from the club's outreach programs. A couple goes through counseling before they get married; the military put their people through a mission briefing before sending them into the field. We should similarly prepare our own prospective members, before they have to make a commitment they might not have understood.

"The next step is to induct them into the club. Contrary to Bob's experience, most club inductions I have witnessed have been quite special events—and so they should be. The new member must be made to feel special—and proud that he or she is entering the worldwide fellowship of Rotary. I have seen clubs even invite the new member's family to be there the day they are inducted.

"But it does not stop there. For at least six months, the new member should be in a program that proactively educates them about the local club and the world of Rotary. You cannot just throw him in and leave him to sink or swim. As another Scottish Rotarian—John Kenny—likes to say: 'A member ignored is a member lost.'"

"In my club, we had a stockbroker join, back in about August or September," said Sue. "By December, he had left Rotary. I ran into him in a store right before Christmas. When he told me he had quit the club, I was shocked, and asked why. He very bluntly told me that he had joined at the suggestion of one of our members, who is a client, and whom, he said, implied the club would be a great source of sales leads. But after—I think he called it something like 'three wasted months'—and no new customers, he left.

"Now, as a club, *we* failed. First, we failed to properly train the member who proposed him.

Second, we failed to properly prepare him for what Rotary is and how Rotarians are supposed to act. Finally, although I thoroughly disagree with his commercial motives for joining the Rotary club, we failed him. His *job* is finding new clients and selling stocks, and who can blame him for pursuing what was represented to him as a sales opportunity? He, too, left because of unmet expectations.

"I read a book called *Sales SuperStars*," Sue continued. "And the author said the key to continued sales success is to not over-promise and under-deliver—as the stereotypical bad salesman does, but to 'Promise a lot—but deliver more.' We have a *lot* to promise in Rotary. We should not allude to benefits that aren't there just so we can make the 'sale' of a new member."

"Your reference to the training program reminded me of something I saw when I was making up at the Rotary Club of Stuart, Florida," said Duncan, looking at me. "They have a four-hour training curriculum for all new members. They assign a half-hour each to the subjects like attendance and makeups, membership, club service, community service, youth service, vocational service, international service, and The Rotary Foundation. They put two of these topics together, and then ask new members to attend a meeting for one hour a month for the first four months in the club. They told me it is extremely effective, not only at retaining members, but at energizing old *and* new members. The entire club seemed to be on the same wavelength."

"You travel a lot, don't you?" Bob asked. "Do you *always* make up at a Rotary club when you're away?"

"Absolutely!" Duncan declared. "In fact, I often visit clubs even though I don't technically need a makeup."

"Why?"

"You see, you're only asking that because, unfortunately, you've never been introduced to the same Rotary I know—and I feel really sad about that, Bob. I have so much fun in my Rotary club, and when I travel, I deliberately visit other clubs because, you know what? They make me feel welcome—and I have fun there, too. Those words we used a lot earlier—fun and fellowship—are *real* in Rotary. Not only do I enjoy their company, but in almost every Rotary club I visit, I learn something new that either enriches me, inspires me, or educates me. I'm in a *great* club, but we don't have all the answers. That is what is so great about being a part of a worldwide network of Rotary clubs. Much of what we do is the same, but I cannot tell you how many times I've seen a club doing something really neat, either a service project that energizes the membership or a program or procedure that makes the club more effective. I have learned from those examples—and often bring ideas back to my home club."

"I think we all can learn from other Rotarians and Rotary clubs," said Sue. "And just the idea exchange we've had tonight is a shining example of that."

CHAPTER 6

Time and Cost

"**H**ugh, the company I work for has gone through a painful process of reorganization over the past year," said Bob. "We've had an intense cost-reduction program, which included about 3,000 layoffs. Many things that were once allowed have now been sacrificed so we can become a leaner, more cost-effective, competitive company.

"Before you joined us, I was telling the others that one of my problems with membership in Rotary is the commitment of time and money it requires. My company no longer pays my dues, and frankly, it is really expensive—especially since they went upscale and moved the meetings to a fancy hotel. So I pay for Rotary from my own pocket—and those meal costs are not even tax deductible. The other issue is the cost of time. I work at a technology campus on the outskirts of town. For me to attend Rotary, I face a 25-minute drive, plus the 90-minute meeting. It is really hard for me to justify being away from the office for two-and-a-half hours in the middle of the work day."

Before Hugh could respond, Sue entered the fray. "I especially agree with him on the cost concern," she added. "In my case, I *am* the company, so the cost of membership comes out of my own pocket. I have a huge problem with those who engineered our move to a 25 percent more-expensive restaurant just so they could eat fancier meals. But I can budget for the weekly dues; what I think scares people is all the extra stuff they get hit with."

"Like what?" I asked.

"Well, we've got the weekly meals, dues to the club, district, and Rotary International," Bob replied. "Then they come around each week selling five-dollar fifty-fifty tickets, and our sergeant-at-arms manages to fine at least five or six people every week—that's usually another five dollars if he catches you. These are fun things, and the individual costs are small, but taken together with meals and parking, they add up. Every three months, we have a fellowship event, such as a dinner and a show—and that can easily amount to $100 per person. The Foundation chairman is quite aggressive about winning district awards for per-capita giving, so I agreed to become a Paul Harris Fellow this year—that's another thousand dollars. I know the money goes to a good cause, but it is tough to be expected to keep shelling out so much—especially as Sarah and I have just bought a new house. Twice in the past couple of months when I attended Rotary, the speaker was from some local organization with really powerful needs: a battered-women's shelter and the Red Cross. Then the club president said that we should rally around these causes and make what he called "personal, sacrificial pledges" to them. They passed around a pad with each member's name on it and asked us to write beside our name the amount we would pledge. Most of the names had $200-$500 beside them by the time it got to me. I'm beginning to think Rotary is a rich person's club; that I must either spend more than I can afford, or feel guilty for *not* doing so."

"I must say, I can see your point," Duncan agreed. "Of course, I'm retired now, so I don't worry about the time issue. But of course, I also have no expense account that picks up my tab. As I travel around and visit other clubs, I do sometimes think, 'Wow! That's quite a financial commitment.' I just made up at the Rotary Club in Los Angeles last week and lunch was $29, plus $7 for parking. I don't know many people who could afford $36 for lunch every week."

"There was some discussion on the board about limiting the number of fund-raising events, but it was defeated," Sue said. "The majority said, 'People can always say *no.*' But it does seem we're always having a raffle or dinner or golf outing—and in addition to our own events, we frequently have visiting Rotarians who pitch their own fund raisers to us. Then there are the district events."

"What do you mean?" asked Hugh.

"Look, don't take offense, Hugh. I know you are the incoming district governor. But sometimes I wonder if your people in the district leadership really understand what it's like for ordinary Rotarians like us." She gestured at Bob and Duncan. "You are constantly urging us to support district events: the Foundation dinner, the district changeover, the district's trip to the international convention, RYLA, the GSE banquet, and the district conference. Have you also noticed that you generally get the same people at every event? I was looking through that booklet on the history of our district a few weeks ago, and the attendance at district conferences has remained essentially static—or declined—for 20 years. Our assistant governor told me we would have around 175 Rotarians at this year's conference. That's an embarrassment! We have, what, 2,100 Rotarians in the district? Fifty-four clubs? That means the major district event of the year—which the governor's entire team has been pushing for twelve months— is being ignored by 93 percent of the membership. Now to my mind, that could only be attributable to three reasons. One, poor marketing—but I think they've done a good job there. Two, people don't care. And I believe there's a general ambivalence toward both club and district activities. That is why we have been discussing the urgent need to energize Rotary tonight. But the third reason is cost. Just look at this weekend's district conference. For two nights' hotel accommodation and a couple of dinners and lunches, by the time you pay for drinks, parking, travel—and the fund-raising tickets in all the hospitality rooms—it will cost between $900 and $1,000 a couple. I could have a weekend in Paris for less than that!"

Poor Hugh looked as if he had been hit in the head with a brick. "I *knew* I should have asked for a table for one when I walked in here," he said, with a grimace. "But let me respond seriously. There are two issues, as I understand you: the commitment of time that Rotary membership requires, and the financial cost of membership—am I right?"

We all agreed.

"Let me address the time part first," he began. "We already talked about the importance of acquainting the prospective member with the time commitment for being a Rotarian. Now let me back up for a moment. I once had a conversation with a club president who told me the owner of one of the most famous baseball teams in America belonged to his club. He went on to admit that they traveled so much that his attendance at club meetings was, at best, sporadic. Under traditional R.I. rules, he would have been ejected from the club for missing four consecutive meetings. He certainly didn't contribute much to, or benefit from, that Rotary fellowship we've just talked about.

"But..." Hugh hesitated, pointing his finger to make the point, "the club president said the member paid his bills on time, he contributed tens of thousands of dollars to club charitable efforts, and whenever they needed anything—such as 100 tickets to a game for disabled kids—the club only had to ask him. Now, let me ask you, was he a bad Rotarian because he did not faithfully spend hours of time volunteering with club projects and attending every meeting?"

"Of course not," I answered, apparently echoing everybody else's opinions, judging from their nods. "But I also must say that he did not do much to energize the club. He was not a *bad* Rotarian, but a 20-member Rotary club with ten people like him would die—regardless of their personal generosity."

"I agree," said Hugh. "So here's the challenge I feel as the incoming district governor: how can I create an environment and attitude that will make people like that baseball team-owner still feel comfortable with being a Rotarian—but perhaps inspire him to become more active? How can I energize the existing members of our clubs to make attendance better, membership more rewarding, and their clubs more active in service projects?"

"You get people more involved," I answered.

"Absolutely! And I'll get to that in a minute. But the second part of my question addresses both the time and the cost issues. How can our clubs structure themselves to become more relevant, attractive, and affordable to people who would make great Rotarians—but don't feel comfortable in our current model?"

"I have an idea," I suggested. "You know, for the better part of a century, Rotary had essentially one format, and all clubs had to fit into it. But today, things are different. None of our core values and beliefs have changed, but R.I. realizes that the business world has. Just as people are different—they are inspired and threatened by different factors—so there are now different Rotary club formats."

"Give us an example," Duncan demanded.

"Okay. For most of my first twenty years in Rotary, there were only two types of club: those that met for lunch, and those that met for dinner. But those meals can be expensive, especially in first-class hotels. Attitudes changed. As Bob said, the old two-hour lunch disappeared. Business people were held to new accountability standards for their time, and in the evening, many wanted to be with their families. So the breakfast club was started, and in recent years, the vast majority of newly chartered Rotary clubs decided to meet early, conduct their business—and still allow their members to be at work by nine o'clock in the morning."

"Not me. I don't do mornings," Bob volunteered.

"Bob, you prove my point," I said. "We in Rotary need to be flexible. Not all people are the same, so all Rotary clubs cannot have the same flavor. They need to understand what their members need. If the *only* clubs were early morning clubs—you would never have joined Rotary."

"Okay, with the conversation going in this generation, I would like to share an idea with you," said Hugh. "It is still a secret, so may I ask you not to say anything about it until you hear the announcement in a month or so?"

Everybody agreed.

"One of my first initiatives after July 1st will be to help start the first sundowner's club in our district. The extension committee has already done their survey, and I think we will begin with at least 25 members."

"What's a sundowner's club?" asked Sue.

"It will meet after work, but before dinner. Right now, the organizing Rotarian has negotiated with the Top Deck restaurant for a meeting room from 5.30 to 6.30 on Mondays. The restaurant said that is the slowest night of the week for banquets, and most parties don't start until 7.30 anyway, so they have given us a great price. The meeting will officially begin at 5.30, and for the first 15 minutes, it will be fellowship time; not a bad way to end the day, if you think about it. Members will pay for their own drinks and the restaurant will provide pitchers of iced tea and lemonade, along with hors d'oeuvres: you know, finger foods, chips, pretzels.

"At 5.45, the bell will ring and people will take their seats. For the first 15 minutes, club business will be conducted, then promptly at six o'clock, the program begins, and just as with most clubs, the speakers will be assigned 20 minutes for their presentation. Remember, nobody has to wait around for dinner to be served—there *is* no meal! At 6.20, the program ends, and there is ten minutes left for the sergeant-at-arms, fifty-fifty drawing, and final announcements before the meeting adjourns at 6.30. One hour—actually, forty-five minutes from gavel-to-gavel—bang!" Hugh slapped his hand on the table so hard we all jumped.

"That's incredible!" said Bob, wide-eyed. "What will it cost?"

"Other than district and R.I. dues, I think the restaurant has quoted them eight or nine dollars a week," he answered.

Bob looked incredulous. *"Nine dollars!* Our lunch alone is now eighteen dollars a week. My club now bills me ninety-five dollars a month. Plus, I *love* the time part. I could be in and out of this meeting without missing work—and I'd still be home in case Sarah and I wanted to do something together that evening."

"Now, wait a minute!" Sue said sternly. "You *promised* to stay in our club so you could be on my leadership team. You can't desert me now."

"That was before I knew about the new sundown Rotary club," he said, defensively.

"So what you are saying is, if Sarah suddenly discovered a younger, better guy, it would be okay to desert you, because she had not known about him when she made her commitment to you?"

Duncan covered his mouth so his smile would not be detected.

"Boy," I thought to myself, for the second time tonight. "She's good."

"You've got me!" said Bob, holding up his hands in the surrender position.

Hugh broke the tension. "Bob, what is it that appeals to you about the new club, and how do you see us marketing it?"

"As I said, I like the fact that its meetings take less time. Frankly, I don't usually eat lunch, and when I do, it's typically a quick sandwich at my desk. For darned sure, it's not a full-course eighteen-dollar hot meal. The second thing I like about it is the cost—in case you couldn't tell!

"As to whom it would appeal? I think people like me. Younger people, fast-track professionals, people in a work environment that makes it difficult to take off for two hours at midday. I think I speak for a lot of people in my position when I say we could justify taking off half a day to mentor kids in the inner-city school, or to work at the food bank. That's because our employers see those activities as good corporate citizenship. But it is more difficult to take off for lunch meetings having nothing to do with the company."

"If I may interject," said Duncan. "We had two wonderful members in my club who resigned—but who I believe would move to the sundown club in a heartbeat. One was a pastor, the other a funeral director. Both men told me how they loved Rotary, but so often had church committee meetings or funerals that started around 7.30; they were constantly having to skip Rotary for that reason and felt they were letting the club down."

"Since even before I became Rotary International President, I was constantly on the road meeting Rotary clubs around the world," I told them. "I must admit, it is very nice—very impressive—to see them meeting in luxury hotels, and to attend district conferences in absolutely fabulous resorts. But we have to be careful not to make Rotary unaffordable to its members—to make it, as one of you said, a rich man's club. We need to cross those barriers and make membership appealing and affordable to everybody that can help us advance our cause.

"Rotary stands for peace in a troubled world. It feeds the hungry, heals the sick, and gives hope to the hopeless. It leads the way in promoting ethical conduct at a time when corruption and scandals seem to make the headlines every day. It works with children and teenagers, and performs extraordinary acts of voluntary service in thirty-thousand communities around the world. Now who can do all those things? Retired men, young women, the barons of industry—and those taking their first steps along their career path. Most importantly, they feel better about themselves—and one another—and have fun as they meet together and work for a better world.

"We need not change *what* Rotary does, but by understanding the needs and concerns of all our potential members, we might need to change *how* we do it—at least, on the club level."

CHAPTER 7

Terms of Engagement

"All those activities are noble pursuits," said Sue. "But you already admitted that some people join Rotary for the wrong reasons. Regardless of their initial rationale for becoming a member, how do you get them involved? I think you said before that there are members of Rotary clubs, and there are Rotarians. That resonated with me. We actually have some new people—and others who have been in the club for years—and they certainly fall into the *members of a Rotary club* category. Since I am coming up to be president, how can I *energize* the club? Not for my own ego's sake, I hasten to add, but so more of our members can discover the joys and rewards of being a *Rotarian*?"

"The best Rotarian is an *involved* Rotarian," I replied. "And I believe the best way to turn a knife-and-fork-club member into a Rotarian is to engage him or her from the very beginning. A Past District Governor from the Vail-Eagle Valley Rotary Club—Eddie Blender—told me what his club does. He said, 'Our club begins gathering at about 7.30 for our 8 a.m. meeting. But I invited ten of the most recent new members to come early for a 6.45 a.m. planning session. They all showed up and in less than a minute I presented a message to them—such as, *Our club usually awards RYLA scholarships to two or three students yearly, but this year, we'd like to send ten—but we don't have the funds available. I need you to figure out how we can send ten. Please appoint a chairperson and let's meet again at the same time in two weeks and let me know how you will raise the funds.*' Not only did they write the plan…they took full ownership and made it happen—and most have become active leaders in the club.

"Assuming you implement the plan we've discussed here tonight, you will have first identified what your club has to offer, and then *whom* you want to recruit as members. Then you will have identified *why* this person wants to join the club; what they expect, what their service 'hot button' is. Is it service to children, or the environment, the club's golf tournament, or perhaps international service?

"Now your club has met with the prospect even before they joined and explained the duties and opportunities that come with being a Rotarian. The candidate—let's call her Chris—joins the club and immediately enters a familiarization program which, over the next few months, will acquaint her with Rotary's history, service opportunities, and projects of both the club and R.I. My good friend Sonny Brown is a past R.I. vice president from El Paso, Texas, and he showed me this wonderful program they have in his district called SPUR:

Special Program for Understanding. SPUR was the brainchild of past district governor Vince Ward, and it has been replicated all over the world."

"What was that again...SPUR?" asked Sue, making a note.

"Yes, SPUR, Special Program for Understanding," I confirmed. "The program's objective is to bring basic Rotary knowledge to new members and old in a concise, condensed format to enable them to be better informed—with the hope that better knowledge will result in more personal involvement. Once per month, members are educated about Rotary's commitment to the Four Avenues of Service, Youth, and Ethics. Other topics include a club's attitude—and a Rotarian's responsibility—in such areas as membership, attendance, financial obligations, and opportunities for involvement."

"Speaking of acronyms, when I attended the International Assembly, I heard about another fantastic program the Rotary Club of El Paso began," Hugh interjected. "They call it STAR—Special Training for Action in Rotary. Within two weeks of joining the club, new members are visited by a knowledgeable Rotarian who invites the new member to a series of special breakfasts. For the next year, they meet as a small group, all new members plus several experienced ones—at a separate time and place from the regular Rotary club meeting. They use this time to build camaraderie, but more importantly, to inform them about every program, project, obligation, and service opportunity the club offers. At the end, they even have a graduation ceremony. Now can you imagine how motivated and informed these members are, and how much better prepared for club leadership—and how much more likely they are to value their membership in Rotary than those new members in clubs with no formal training programs?"

I smiled as I thought of how many times other Rotary clubs had told me how they had since adopted the STAR program with similar positive results. "Let's go back to our imaginary new member," I said. "Remember now, the key is to get Chris involved quickly. I know of many clubs that make new members a greeter at the weekly meetings for their first few months so they come to know—and become known by—other members. The Rotary Club of San Francisco even has an informal group the call the Forty-Niners. Of course, theirs is a large club, and they take the 49 most recent members to join and that group arranges social and service events outside the regular club meetings. When the next person joins the club, the person who now joined 50 members ago leaves the Forty-Niners—but by that time, they have really become acquainted with, and attached to, the Rotary Club. You see, for Chris—or those San Francisco members, to those new to any club—to feel warmly welcomed, it is essential that she has a sense of connection to its members and activities.

"Other clubs have had great success integrating new recruits into active participation with a mentoring program. "I'll talk about that later," I said, jotting down a note to remind myself. "But let's get back to Chris. She is now a member of the club, she is getting to know the other members and they are getting to know her. She enjoys coming to Rotary, and the familiarization program is validating her decision to join; she previously had no idea what a history of community service this organization has. At some point during the recruitment process, you should have asked Chris to complete an Inventory of Interests [see Appendix A]. This allows you to identify the specific areas in which she is most interested in helping, once she has become a Rotarian. Your club should also have an up-to-date printed Inventory of Club Activities, on which is listed every single opportunity for members to serve. From *fund-raising* to *club bulletin* to *public relations* and *children's literacy project*—put everything on a form and at least twice a year ask every member to select those activities where they would like to help.

"So, back to Chris. You notice that on her Inventory of Interests form, she checked *club bulletin* and *children's literacy project*. In talking with her, you discover she has a passion for children—and for three years wrote the newsletter when she was active in the Parent-Teachers Association. How better to increase a new member's feeling of enjoyment and self-worth than to let them help in an area in which they are interested? Either her mentor or (depending on the club's size) the club service director or president goes to the chair of the children's literacy project and says, 'Look, we've got a new member here who wants to help on your committee. You need to contact her while she is still enthusiastic and get her involved. When would you like to do that?' Then you do the same with the club bulletin committee.

"Remember, we are all volunteers. We also share the common goal of making good things happen through our Rotary club. So who would not welcome more help in their area?"

"What if the existing chairperson felt threatened by the new member's enthusiasm and ideas?" Duncan asked.

"Of course, we are all human beings, we are all subject to human personality traits," I reasoned. "But we are also all Rotarians; we subscribe to the motto *Service Above Self.* Put yourselves in that position. You've been working hard all year on a particular project that is near and dear to your heart, and now another Rotarian who shares your interests offers to help. Why wouldn't you welcome that? Again, we all have different personalities, but unless the new member went charging in with an attitude of 'You're doing this all wrong. Let me show you how to do it,' I cannot imagine the existing committee wouldn't welcome Chris with open arms."

"I agree that the new member should not propose changing everything overnight," said Hugh. "But they can also bring a fresh perspective and innovation to a project. I know of one club whose weekly bulletin was a miserable-looking thing. It was simply a typed one-page sheet of paper with three or four sentences listing last week's speaker, this week's menu—and little else. A new member who, by profession, was a writer, joined the club, and he indicated a willingness to help with the bulletin. Producing the weekly missive had been a real chore for the incumbent writer, so when she detected the enthusiasm from this new chap, she suggested *he* take the lead role and she would back him up wherever needed. Within a month, there was a new club bulletin. The front and back covers were in color, and every week the contents were filled with news, humor, information on club projects, a little 'focus on' sidebar alternately describing a Rotary historical fact or a member's biography. The club president told me, 'Our members cannot wait to read the bulletin when they arrive every week. Those who miss a meeting ask the secretary to mail them the bulletin.

"The story gets better. The new member loved writing the bulletin. When I heard about it, I was an assistant governor, and I proposed his name to the district newsletter committee. He has since become very involved in district and club affairs. He will lead our Group Study Exchange team to Turkey this year—and all this came about because his club found out what he liked doing and then they got him involved from the very beginning of his membership."

I thought of another young Rotarian I know who joined a Rotary club. He reminded me a little of Bob, because he was in his late twenties—probably less than half the average age of the other members. He could have easily felt out of place and walked away, but another member, who was only a few years older, asked him to be his assistant chairman of the annual parade which the club staged at Halloween. The assignment caused him to interact with every club member, bring some innovative ideas to the 30-year-old community event, and his enthusiasm and leadership endeared him to the other club members. He went on to become club president, helped charter two new Rotary clubs, and chaired several district committees.

"When I was in the district governor training program, I heard so many good ideas from other clubs and districts," Hugh continued. "I remember a PDG from Grass Valley, Texas, telling me that his club has six teams, each of which is responsible for providing the program, pledge of allegiance, greeters, newsletter, and introduction of visiting Rotarians for two months each year. Those team members are also assigned to a committee with the Four Avenues of Service. So any time a new member comes into the club, he or she is just assigned to one of those teams. Can you imagine how it is *impossible* for them not to feel involved with Rotary from the very beginning?"

Memories of examples proving the values of engaging new Rotarians in meaningful service early in their Rotary journey streamed into my mind. A vivid example was John Colville of Paramount, California. He joined Rotary so give something back to the community that had provided him with a living, and yet he languished in his Rotary club for two years without anybody involving him in any meaningful service. He told me he was disenchanted and on the point of dropping out, when somebody asked him to take over as club president. A few years later, he was nominated for district governor and went on to lead the Rotary clubs in the Los Angeles area with pride and distinction—yet Rotary almost lost that faithful servant because we did not engage him in our program. I have sat on too many committees, heard testimony from too many club and district officers, and am absolutely convinced of the imperative to get new members involved in the club as soon as they join.

"I don't want this to be a conversation where we seem to be going back and forth with 'I can top that' anecdotes," I said. "But I just remembered another example that corroborates your point, Hugh. There's a Rotarian named Marion Banks at the Rotary Club of Dunwoody, Georgia. She started an AIDS awareness and education program in the public schools that became so popular, it spread across the whole state, generating very positive public relations for her Rotary club. New members—sometimes, even husband and wife teams—have joined the Rotary Club of Dunwoody just so they can work in its AIDS awareness program, because they care so much about the problem and saw Rotary as the vehicle that allowed them to help."

"But Dunwoody, Georgia, must be a large club if it can launch a statewide program," argued Bob. "What if we do start this new sundowners club...there might only be twenty members at first, and if you consider that no club will ever garner one hundred percent support from its members, how can you launch a project that is impressive enough to attract attention—and new people?"

"You can partner with other small clubs," I answered. "Let me give you an example. Four small Rotary clubs in Ohio decided they could do an international service project more effectively if they pooled their resources, than they could be acting separately. Bob Kluck, a past district governor who is a member of one of those clubs told me, 'Small dreams don't inspire, large dreams do!' So the clubs recruited members from their agricultural area to visit the Tarahumara Indians in México to help them cope with the crop failures they were enduring from a persistent drought. They returned to Ohio and motivated their fellow Rotarians to raise enough to buy an ambulance, fill it with medical equipment, and send it to an impoverished hospital in Creel, México. The interest and enthusiasm among those Rotarians is so high that they are now planning another humanitarian trip to provide safe-water wells.

"Now, that's an example of clubs combining their resources. But in Clover Park, Washington, the Rotary club adopted a local school, where its members volunteer to have lunch and read to young children. How compelling—and how easy— do you think it is to persuade new members to take an hour every now and again and do that?

"Nothing cements a new member's commitment to their Rotary club so well as to get them involved in a hands-on volunteerism project. Sometimes that new member will take the initiative, but we cannot take the chance of being passive about this. Remember, we are looking for ways to *energize* our existing clubs and improve *retention* of new members. And today, in addition to its own programs, Rotary partners with organizations such as CBMI, RotaPlast, and Sightsavers—so the opportunities for volunteerism are unlimited.

"A friend of mine in San Antonio, Texas, told me that in his club, 'Each new member is encouraged to participate in a community hands-on project in the first four months of membership. The involvement allows them to meet other members beyond the social setting of the club meetings. It emphasizes the service pledge of Rotary and brings personal commitment. That personal participation is the seed for the need to belong to Rotary as an organization bigger than themselves. I did not understand what Rotary was all about until I built a playground along with forty other Rotarians. Until then, it was a weekly luncheon with my business associates.'"

"*That's* the Rotary club I want to belong to," said Bob.

"That is the Rotary club I want to be president of—and which I want you to help me in," said Sue, reaching over and tapping his shoulder.

CHAPTER 8

What Else May I Help You With?

I suddenly became aware of the waitress standing behind my right shoulder; I looked up as she asked, "What else may I help you with?" I gestured to my four colleagues. They all indicated they did not want anything. "Just the check, please," I told her.

"That was an interesting question," Duncan observed.

"What was?"

"The one the waitress just asked: 'What else may I help you with?'" he replied. "I've been watching and listening to the proceedings tonight. Before I met you, Frank, I don't think the words *Rotary club* meant much to me. I certainly could not have given an accurate definition of what a Rotary club does. It seems to me that I have been blessed by joining a really great club. From the very day I joined, the other members embraced me, made me feel welcome, and put me to work. I have a sense of having accomplished much more for my community through Rotary than I ever could have by myself.

"I guess I am still influenced by my experiences from spending a long career with a large multinational corporation. I am impressed that you, a past worldwide president of Rotary, would carve an entire evening out of your busy schedule to sit here, giving advice to three new Rotarians you barely know. All through the evening, your attitude reflected the waitress's question: 'What else may I help you with?' You could be up in your room sleeping off the effects of your long flight; you could be hob-nobbing with a group of your old PDG friends—but you are *here*, with us. I guess my question is, why, Frank?"

I breathed in deeply as I considered my reply. "Because I really care about Rotary," I began. "I don't want this to sound melodramatic or cliché-filled, but Rotary has had a profound effect on my life. Most of my friends are those I've made through Rotary. I have traveled to maybe 125 countries and seen absolutely incredible examples of lives being saved, diseases healed, poverty solved, education improved, and suffering eliminated—all by Rotarians. I simply don't have enough words—in English or Spanish—to tell you how much the world needs a vibrant Rotary, and how much *people* need the fun, fellowship, service opportunities, and personal enrichment that comes from being a real Rotarian.

"So when I see young guys like Bob—who can give so much to, and receive so much from Rotary, I grieve. And Sue, who has all the right combination of leadership skills, charisma, and enthusiasm to guide her club to new levels of excellence—when I hear she is so frustrated that she is thinking of walking away from Rotary, and then I feel *compelled* to help. So the waitress asks, 'What else may I help you with?' And I suppose you are right, that *has* become my question too—but in a way it is every Rotarian's question.

"I want to help you two because I know how good life can be as a member of a dynamic, energized Rotary club. And I have seen that clubs which don't have community service projects, regular, interesting programs, and membership involvement are those that will gradually decline and even fold. Is that one of the saddest things imaginable? Especially when their communities *need* those Rotary clubs—and the alternative: healthy, vibrant, service-active Rotary clubs—is so easy to attain.

"So how do we wrap this up with a meaningful plan? Actually, I think we should start with the bad news. Let's prepare an exit questionnaire, and any time a member resigns from the club, we should ask them to complete it. As a matter of fact, why not go back to every person who has left the club over, say, the past two years, and ask them to fill it out. It is important to know why they left. Look at Bob, he has all the makings of a super Rotarian, but he almost slipped away—and your club would never have known why. After you have reviewed these exit questionnaires, look for common themes in the answers. What if not only Bob, but ten other members had left the club over the past year, all of whom had cited 'cost of membership' as reasons? You cannot control some causes of membership loss, such as relocation or death—but you sure can eliminate others, if you find they are becoming common complaints.

"Now you know the primary reasons why your members leave your club, you can focus on how to structure it to be more dynamic, effective, and energetic. You have done a club inventory, you know your strengths, you know your existing members, and you have identified your target audience of prospective future members.

"As you attract those new members into the club, you use a formal plan that educates them as to their expectations, responsibilities, and volunteerism opportunities. You go far beyond the practice of saying 'Here's your pin and first month's bill. Welcome to Rotary,' as was Bob's sad experience. Instead, you help them feel *part* of the club by adopting a proactive assimilation plan—such as making them a greeter, and putting them on an active committee right away.

"Mentoring programs work extremely well. I have seen clubs pair up new members with experienced Rotarians. I know that the Rotary Club of Newark, Ohio, requires new members to have two sponsors, and one of those sponsors becomes the applicant's mentor after he or she joins the club. The mentor could be the person who sponsors them into the club, or it might be somebody in the same vocation, age group, residential neighborhood, or field of interest as that new member. There are many variations of mentoring programs. Mentors sometimes agree to car pool to the meeting with their mentee, and to introduce them to other members, to explain certain things about the club's history, programs, and mission. If the new member misses a meeting, their mentor often drops by their home or office with a copy of the club bulletin, and I have seen the mentor offer to accompany them to a convenient nearby club to experience a makeup. Bill Cadwallader, an old Rotary friend in Cortland, New York, advocates that the mentor 'give words of encouragement even up to the time the new member becomes club president and beyond.' His point is, 'We never outgrow our appreciation of someone special to give a word of encouragement and congratulations...it should be the beginning of a lifelong special relationship between two friends in the family of Rotary.'

"Speaking of family, I cannot overemphasize the importance of involving the Rotarian's *family* in their Rotary experience. Now, you may ask the question, 'Why? My wife isn't going to be the Rotarian; I am. Why do I need to involve her, or my children, in Rotary from the outset?' There are so many demands on our time nowadays and sometimes, your Rotary activities might conflict with family time. By letting them see how important your involvement with Rotary is—to the community, your profession, and the world—they are far more likely to accept the value and your benefits that come with your Rotary membership.

"I suggest you invite the new members' immediate family to participate in their induction into the club, and even before that, to include them at the time you brief the prospect on the meaning of membership in Rotary. Some of the clubs with the strongest membership retention are those that have frequent outings, dinners, and even joint service projects for members and their spouses and partners. That spouse is far more likely to urge the Rotarian to stay in the club if they themselves understand and support what Rotary represents.

"We are in a fast-track world today. People on the one hand expect meetings to be active, rapid-paced, and interesting. On the other hand, they are so used to impersonal service and hours on end of interaction with nothing more personal than a computer screen that Rotary membership can hold for them the promise of fun, friendship, and the ability to do something meaningful.

"One hundred years ago, Rotary's founder, Paul Harris, understood this need for fellowship, and it was the number one reason why he started our organization. Today, that basic human need still exists. Some of the ways we operate clubs have changed—and we need some of them to still make those changes—but the ideals and rewards of membership have not."

"You said more changes need to be made. What sort of changes are you referring to?" asked Duncan.

"We have talked about several of them tonight," answered Sue. "Look! I've made enough notes to write a book." She began reeling off suggestions from her list:

Avoid cliques
Make meetings fun
Conduct a pre-membership questionnaire
Involve them right away

Educate them about Rotary
Rotary fellowship groups
Always have interesting programs
Watch the time
Keep it affordable,
Let new people try new things
Make a target list of prospective members
Find out why members leave
Involve families

"I mentioned my friend Bob Menconi before," I continued. "He likes to compare Rotary with a department store: when you walk into a big shop like that, you are more interested in some departments than in others. Rotary is like that. It is so large we must accept that members are vitally interested in some areas but not at all motivated by others. The bond that ties us together is the *ideal* of service, the *concept* of volunteerism, of giving back, of making a difference. But as a Rotary leader, I must be aware that the customers in my department store are not all shopping for the same thing. I am passionately committed to Rotary's Avoidable Blindness Campaign, but if all I do during the year I am club president is push Avoidable Blindness, I will likely turn some members off. Because Sue here may be more interested in RYLA [Rotary Youth Leadership Award] and Bob wants to focus on mentoring at-risk kids and Duncan's 'thing' is service to the elderly.

"The bottom line—and excuse the cliche —is that while some people may have joined Rotary for the prestige or the networking potential, the most sustainable reason we can offer them is to anticipate their question, 'How can I make a difference?'—and the show them the answer.

"If you cannot answer that—or if you haven't even taken the time to ask the question—your members will vote with their feet. But you need to do as Stephen Covey urges as another of his *7 Habits of Highly Effective People*: 'Begin with the end in mind.' If you can know what your members want, provide for those needs, and make attendance at Rotary more fun and rewarding than whatever other activities in their lives are competing for that time period each week—then you have proactive leadership that will lead to a growing, and loyal, membership base."

Duncan yawned, which promptly set of a yawn from Hugh.

"I'm sorry, Frank," he said. "I wasn't yawning at you. I've been up since 5.30."

"Don't worry," I assured him. "Look, we all have an early start at the conference tomorrow. So let me close with a final thought. You have all made notes of our conversation tonight, and several of you have commented on this or that good idea. But ideas without action are worthless. People go to international conventions, district conferences, PETS [President Elects' Training Seminar] and so on all the time and take notes. Then they go home full of the best *intentions* to change, to implement those ideas—but do nothing. Years later, those notes are covered with dust in a yellowing file folder.

"At the end of his seminar on leadership development, Dave Forward tells this story:

'Once upon a time, a bunch of turkeys attended a seminar called *How to Fly*. For two days, they studied principles of aerodynamics, the relationship of drag to lift, methods of propulsion, and avoiding midair collisions. They took copious notes, they broke into small study groups, they asked all the right questions and scored well in the written exam. At four o'clock on the last day, the seminar instructor took all the turkeys to the roof of the conference center and made them jump off.

'It worked! They swooped and soared and banked and dove, and for the first time in their lives, they didn't feel like turkeys— they felt like *eagles*! The instructor congratulated each one of them as he handed them their graduation certificates.

'And then they all walked home.'

"Hugh, have the courage to be bold as district governor next year. Be more influenced by the *possibilities* than what past governors insist are the traditions. Sue, think outside the box as club president. Your most important job is to motivate new and existing members by making your meetings meaningful to them. Remember what Albert Schweitzer once said: 'Example is not the best way of leading others—it is the *only* way.'

"Bob, we need you in Rotary. Quitting would not have helped anything. It is great that you agreed to stay and work with Sue. Now I challenge you to think of this as *your* Rotary club. Take ownership of it. Start thinking of whom you can bring in as new members, and how, when you see a problem, you can be a part of the solution.

"In the final analysis, we are largely responsible for our own destinies and what we get out of life. If we want to leave Rotary because things are not the way we want them, that is our decision, but will the world—or even our own lives—be any the better for that choice? We could always leave one club and join another—one infused with the fellowship and energy we crave, but I believe that should be our *last* resort, not our first. The best choice, I believe, is to be the potter with a piece of clay. Mold it; shape it into something beautiful so that when it is set, you will know that your hands helped create a thing of wonder."

Inventory of Interests

This inventory of interests will help your mentor recommend club committees and activities for you to become involved with. You should complete this form and return it to your mentor.

Name: _____

Classification: _____

Profession: _____

I would like my family to be involved in club activities: ❑ Yes ❑ No

Skills I would like to use: _____

_____

Amount of time I can devote (per week): _____

Please check the topics that interest you.

Community Service
- ❑ Children
- ❑ Disabled persons
- ❑ Environmental issues
- ❑ Health care
- ❑ Literacy and numeracy
- ❑ Population issues
- ❑ Poverty and hunger
- ❑ Urban concerns
- ❑ Other _____

International Service
- ❑ International service projects
- ❑ Other _____

Vocational Service
- ❑ Vocational service projects
- ❑ Other: _____

Club Administration
- ❑ Club bulletin
- ❑ Club programs
- ❑ Fellowship
- ❑ Fundraising
- ❑ Internet/Web page
- ❑ Membership
- ❑ Public relations
- ❑ The Rotary Foundation
- ❑ Other: _____
- ❑ Other: _____
- ❑ Other: _____

(Excerpted from *New Member Orientation*, RI publication # 414-EN)

Resigning Member Questionnaire

We regret that you are leaving our club. This questionnaire will help us assess your satisfaction with your experience as a member of our club. The information you provide will benefit current and future club members. Please return the completed questionnaire to the club secretary.

Why are you leaving our club? (Please mark all that apply)

- ❑ Relocating to a new community
- ❑ Lack of time
- ❑ Competing priorities
- ❑ Financial constraints
- ❑ My fellowship expectations were not met

- ❑ My service expectations were not met
- ❑ My networking expectations were not met
- ❑ Did not feel included
- ❑ Other _____

_____

If you are moving, would you consider joining a Rotary club in your new place of residence or occupation? ❑ Yes ❑ No

Did you feel welcome in our Rotary club? ❑ Yes ❑ No
If no, why not? (Please mark all that apply)
- ❑ I felt demographically isolated: (Please mark/circle all reasons that apply)
  Other members were older / younger / different gender / different ethnicity.
  - ❑ Other demographic reason _____
  - ❑ I did not make an effort to meet other members.
  - ❑ Other members did not make an effort to interact with me.

Did you feel comfortable sharing concerns with club leaders? ❑ Yes ❑ No
If no, why not? (Please mark all that apply)
- ❑ Club leaders had so many responsibilities, I did not want to burden them.
- ❑ Club leaders had their own agenda and were not interested in other ideas.
- ❑ I was not a member long enough to feel comfortable approaching club leaders.
- ❑ I did not want to be perceived as a complainer.
- ❑ Other _____

Did you participate in club projects and activities? ❑ Yes ❑ No

How did you become involved? ❑ I volunteered ❑ I was asked

I was very satisfied / satisfied / dissatisfied with my participation in club activities and projects. (Please circle the appropriate response.)

If you were dissatisfied, why? (Please mark all that apply)

❑ Insufficient knowledge
❑ Personality conflicts
❑ Cost
❑ Personal time conflicts

❑ Lack of resources
❑ Lack of support from other members
❑ Insufficient family involvement
❑ Other

How do you feel about the level of our club's involvement in the following types of activities?

Activity	Level of Club Involvement			
Membership Development	❑ Excessive	❑ Adequate	❑ Insufficient	❑ Not Aware
Member Orientation	❑ Excessive	❑ Adequate	❑ Insufficient	❑ Not Aware
Local Service Projects	❑ Excessive	❑ Adequate	❑ Insufficient	❑ Not Aware
International Service Projects	❑ Excessive	❑ Adequate	❑ Insufficient	❑ Not Aware
Club Public Relations	❑ Excessive	❑ Adequate	❑ Insufficient	❑ Not Aware
Fundraising	❑ Excessive	❑ Adequate	❑ Insufficient	❑ Not Aware
The Rotary Foundation	❑ Excessive	❑ Adequate	❑ Insufficient	❑ Not Aware
Fellowship	❑ Excessive	❑ Adequate	❑ Insufficient	❑ Not Aware

How do you feel about the following additional costs associated with membership in our club?

Type of Cost	Perception of Cost		
Club dues	❑ Excessive	❑ Reasonable	❑ Inadequate
Cost of weekly meetings	❑ Excessive	❑ Reasonable	❑ Inadequate
Amount of club fines/assessments	❑ Excessive	❑ Reasonable	❑ Inadequate
Voluntary contributions to service projects	❑ Excessive	❑ Reasonable	❑ Inadequate
Voluntary contributions to The Rotary Foundation	❑ Excessive	❑ Reasonable	❑ Inadequate

Did you enjoy our weekly meetings? ❑ Yes ❑ No

Please circle the appropriate response in the following questions:
The amount of Rotary content in our meetings was
Adequate / Excessive / Insufficient.
The length of our meetings was Adequate / Excessive / Insufficient.
Our club should have held more / same amount / fewer fellowship activities.
Our club bulletin contained sufficient / excessive / insufficient Rotary information.
Our club bulletin was (please circle all that apply)
interesting / useful / informative / boring / limited / uninformative.
Our meetings were well organized / poorly organized.
Our meeting time was convenient / inconvenient.
   ❑ Suggestion for change (if appropriate) _____
The location of our meeting was convenient / inconvenient.
   ❑ If inconvenient, suggestion for a different venue _____
Which of the following aspects of our meeting place do you find to be unsatisfactory? (Mark all that apply)
❑ Service   ❑ Décor/atmosphere
❑ Meal quality   ❑ Meal variety
❑ Parking availability   ❑ Safety of the area in which it is located
❑ Other _____

Suggestion(s) for change
The following changes would improve club meetings:
❑ Better speakers   ❑ More focus on fellowship
❑ Increased variety of program   ❑ Increased emphasis on vocational
   topics   information
❑ More involvement of family   ❑ Better time management
❑ More service opportunities   ❑ More leadership opportunities

How did your spouse/partner/family feel about your involvement in Rotary?
❑ Proud of my involvement   ❑ Felt it took too much of my time
❑ Wanted to know more/be involved   ❑ Felt it was too expensive
❑ Sought interaction with other Rotary spouses/partners/families
❑ Other _____

Is there anything that our club could have done differently to meet your needs?

_____

Would you like us to contact the Rotary club in your new place of residence to notify them that you are interested in joining their club? ❑ Yes ❑ No

New place of residence:
City   State/Province   Country

Thank you for taking the time to complete this questionnaire and for your commitment to improving our club.

(Adapted from Rotary International document. Used with RI permission)

APPENDIX C

Rotary Fellowship Groups

The following is a list of the Rotary Fellowships. Because new groups are frequently added, it is suggested that you check online at www.Rotary.org.

Medical/Health-related Fellowships

1. Rotarian Fellowship for Fighting AIDS.
2. International Fellowship of Rotarians affected by Hearing Loss.
3. Rotarian Fellowship of Multiple Sclerosis Awareness (FMSA)
4. Post Polio Survivors & Associates Fellowship.
5. International Fellowship of Rotarians with Repaired Hearts (IFRRH).

Recreational Fellowships

1. International Fellowship of Rotarian Amateur Astronomers (IFRAA)
2. Rotarians of Amateur Radio (ROAR)
3. Antique, Classic, and Historic Automobile Fellowship of Rotarians
4. Collectors of Automobile Registration Tags from Around the Globe (CARTAG)
5. Rotarians International Fellowship of Ballroom Dancing
6. International Fellowship of Bird-Watching Rotarians
7. International Fellowship of Bridge Playing Rotarians
8. International Fellowship of Canoeing Rotarians (IFCR)
9. International Caravanning Fellowship of Rotarians (ICFR)
10. International Chess Fellowship of Rotarians (ICFR)
11. International Computer Users Fellowship of Rotarians
12. International Curling Fellowship of Rotarians
13. International Fellowship of Cricket Loving Rotarians
14. Rotarian Fellowship of Cycling to Serve
15. Fellowship of Dog Owning Rotarians (FIDO)
16. Rotarian World Fellowship of Egyptology

17. International Esperanto Fellowship of Rotarians (RADE)
18. International Fellowship of Fishing Rotarians (IFFR)
19. Rotarian International Fellowship of Floral Designers (RIFFD)
20. International Fellowship of Flying Rotarians (IFFR)
21. International Genealogy and Heraldry Fellowship of Rotarians (IGHFR)
22. International Go Playing Fellowship of Rotarians (GPFR)
23. International Golfing Fellowship of Rotarians (IGFR)
24. Rotarians' Recreational Fellowship for Handicrafts
25. Rotary's Global History Fellowship
26. International Home Exchange Fellowship of Rotarians
27. Rotarians Fellowship of Touring Horseback Riders
28. Rotary Automobile License Plate Collectors Fellowship (CARTAG)
29. International Fellowship of Rotarian Magicians (FORM)
30. International Fellowship of Magna Graecia (IFMG)
31. International Fellowship of Motorcycling Rotarians (Rotacyclists)
32. International Mountain Climbing and Hiking Fellowship of Rotarians
33. International Fellowship of Rotarian Musicians (IFRM)
34. Petanque Fellowship of Rotarians
35. International Fellowship of Pre-Colombian Civilizations
36. Rotarian Fellowship of Quilters & Fiber Artists
37. International Fellowship of Railroading Rotarians
38. Recreational Vehicles Fellowship of Rotarians
39. Rotarians-on-the-Internet (ROTT)
40. Rotary Heritage and History Fellowship of Rotarians
41. International Fellowship of Rotary-on-Stamps (ROS)
42. International Fellowship of Running and Fitness Rotarians (IFRFR)
43. International Fellowship of Scouting Rotarians (IFSR)
44. International Skiing Fellowship of Rotarians
45. International Fellowship of Rotarian Sport Divers (IFRSD)
46. International Travel and Hosting Fellowship (ITHF)
47. Rotarians' World Fellowship of Wine Appreciation
48. International Yachting Fellowship of Rotarians
49. Rotarians' International Fellowship of Yoga.

Vocational Fellowships

1. Accountants/CPA Chartered Vocational Fellowship
2. Arts and Communication Vocational Fellowships
3. International Fellowship of Disaster Managers and Responders
4. International Fellowship of Rotarian Editors and Publishers
5. Vocational Fellowship Education-Secondary
6. Vocational Fellowship Education-Special Education
7. Rotarians' International Vocational Fellowship of Engineering and Applied Sciences (RFEAS)
8. Rotarian Vocational Fellowship of Environment
9. Rotarian Fellowship of Eye Care Professionals
10. Finance/Banking Vocational Fellowships
11. Fine Arts and Antiques Vocational Fellowship
12. Vocational Fellowship of Law
13. International Fellowship of Retired and Active Duty Military Personnel
14. Rotarians Fellowship of International Nurses
15. Paper Industry Vocational Fellowship
16. Rotarians' International Fellowship of the Performing Arts (RIFPA)
17. International Pharmacology Fellowship of Rotarians
18. International Fellowship of Rotary Physicians
19. International Fellowship of Rotarian Plastic Surgeons
20. Police/Law Enforcement Professionals Fellowship of Rotarians
21. Poultry Vocational Fellowship of Rotarians (PVFR)
22. Rotarian Fellowship of Psychiatry/Psychology
23. Stockbrokers/Securities Vocational Fellowship
24. Tire Industry Vocational Fellowship
25. Rotarians' International Vocational Fellowship of Total Quality Management
26. Rotarians' International Fellowship of Travel Agents
27. Venture Capital Vocational Fellowship
28. Veterinary Science Vocational Fellowship

Special Interest Fellowships

1. Fellowship of Rotarians for Mine Action
2. Rotarian Fellowship for Population and Development

(List accurate to February 2004)

APPENDIX D

Thanks for the Great Ideas!

Rotary is a global movement of 1.2 million members in 30,000 local Rotary clubs in more than 160 countries and geographic regions. No one club, district, or country has the franchise on the best way to run a Rotary club. Indeed, one of the great strengths that becomes evident at international Rotary meetings is that we can all learn something from the way our fellow Rotarians operate their clubs and serve their communities in faraway lands.

This book is not the exclusive brilliance of its two authors, but rather the collective experience they have witnessed from visiting thousands of Rotary clubs in countless countries. But just as important, it includes the proven ideas of many more Rotarians—some grass-roots members, others senior Rotary International leaders—who enthusiastically responded to the call to make membership retention more effective.

The following is a list of just those whom we know contributed to Frank Talk II. We thank them for their ideas—along with those who made suggestions but omitted their names.

Luis Enrque Acevedo	Bill Cadwallader
Gus Annokkee	Kenneth R. Caplin
Okechukwu Arikibe	Rae Carpenter
R. Asokan	Victor M. Casaretto
	Frank Ceil
Gladys C. Baisa	A. S. Chandrashekar
Jim Berg	Federico Compean
Edward 'Eddie' Blender	Joe Coons
Henry MacD Bodman	Phil Crawford
Don Bowater	Talee Crowe
Sarah Bownds	
Irving J. 'Sonny' Brown	Jennifer Deters
Terry L. Brown	Cliff Dochterman
Marion Bunch	
Charlie Buttke	

John Eberhard
Charles V. Elizondo
Robert Ellis
Rudy Estrellado

Harold Friend

Neil Garber
Fernando Garcia
John Germany
Riaz ul Hassan Ghauri
Mariana Ghersi
Clara Gillard
Elizabeth Giraud
Abe Gordon
Sam Greene
T. D. Griley

Mike Hayes
Teko Hlapo
Dave Hossler
Tom Hughes

Edmilson Inacio

John Kenny
Brian Key
Dennis Klainberg
Bob Kuck, II
Charles Kurtzman

Marge Lamberte
Jorma Lampén
Bob Lanken
Des Lawson

Maureen McDaniel
Donna McDonald

Jerry Meigs
Hector Gerardo Menchaca
Bob Menconi

Hap Mills
James Montgomery
Frank C. Murray

Gene Pankey
Ron Pavellas
Friedrich Chr. Perker
Lou Picconi

Barry Rassin
Bob Rees
Sigfrido Cuen Rodelo
Mark Ruleman
Robert S. Ryan

Angela M. Rester Samse
Harriet Schloer
Robert Scott
M. K. Panduranga Setty
Leah W. Ewing Shaw
Michael Slevnik
Anita Stangl
Bill Sturgeon
Miecislau Surek

Ray Taylor
Karen Teichman
Elias Thomas, III
Barry Thompson
Kenneth D. Tuck

Luis Felipe Valenzuela
Paul Van Nest
Rosa Ma Acevedo de Vasquez
Danny L. Vicencio
Alfredo Elias Pérez Vivas

Lauren Walthour
Wilf Wilkinson

Lucho Zuloaga

Appendix E

The S.T.A.R. Program
Special Training for Action in Rotary

This program was designed by the Rotary Club of El Paso, Texas, USA to whom we gratefully acknowledge permission for inclusion in this book.

1. Upon joining the Rotary Club of El Paso, each new member, whether an active or honorary, or a former member of another Rotary club, is placed on the **STAR** Committee.

New members are requested to fill out a complete questionnaire about themselves and provide a photo. Their biographical sketch is used to introduce the new member and is printed in the club's weekly bulletin.

Each new member has a Red Star pasted on their Rotary Badge and a Red Ribbon attached, identifying them as a **NEW** member. During regular club meetings, older members are encouraged to sit at the table with them to become acquainted. Often the Club President will ask the new members to stand to be identified.

2. The Chairman and/or Co-Chairman of **STAR** Committee visit each new member personally at their place of business within two weeks of becoming a club member for a short orientation meeting.

3. **STAR Breakfast** meetings, the most important aspect of the program, are held once a month on the last Wednesday of every month, except in December. Meetings start promptly at 7:00 a.m. and adjournment is promised by 8:00 a.m.

4. **All** new members expected to attend the **STAR** committee meetings for one year and are charged a non-refundable fee ($75.00), upon joining, for the breakfast meals for their **STAR** year.

5. The Club's Board may elect to grant attendance credit at **STAR** as a Committee Meeting for any club member who wishes go attend.

6. The **STAR** Committee is made up of: Chairman (usually a PDG or past president), Co-Chairman (the immediate past president of the Club), and other members who are past presidents, president-elect and a few carry-over **STAR** members, who may request to remain on the committee.

7. **ALL** of the members of the club are invited to attend at any time to update themselves on Rotary Information and to meet the new members. **In addition**, members of any other clubs in the community or district are welcome to attend.

8. Typical programs begin with:
   - Welcome to first time attendees
   - Congratulations to those who have graduated, or will graduate, from the program.
   - Club announcements and plans
   - Upcoming events in club and district
   - Presentation of the program of the day followed by questions and answers.

9. The *SPUR BOOKLET* (**S**pecial **P**rogram for **U**nderstanding **R**otary) is used as a guide for the programs. Listed are the sequence of programs for a typical **STAR** year:

July	District RYLA Camp	January	Youth Ex Program*
August	Club Treasurer's Report	February	4-Way Test Presentation
September	Club Service	March	Attendance
October	Vocational Service	April	Community Service
November	International Service	May	History of Club
December	No Meeting (HOLIDAY LUNCHEON)	June	Rotary Foundation

* Youth Exchange Students are invited as guests once or twice a year and generally give one of the programs.

10. The new members of the **STAR** Committee are given the responsibility of organizing the "Holiday Luncheon" in December, which honors spouses during the holiday period.

11. **STAR Make-up** meetings are presented once a month immediately after the regular Rotary Luncheon. Such a meeting does not usually take over one half-hour.

12. The **STAR** Committee Chairman publishes a report of the committee breakfast meeting once per month in the weekly club bulletin.

ADVANTAGES OF THE STAR PROGRAM

The annual turnover of **NEW** members allows the repeat of the program every year in the same sequence. All presenters of monthly topics are usually Directors or Committee Chairman of the area of responsibility to be presented.

Besides being an avenue for Rotary Information, the **STAR** Breakfasts acquaint the new members with a few of the older club leaders and all the new members, immediately.

The friendly informality of the small group leads to more questions and good discussions. In a large club it is very helpful for it promotes strong fellowship and a sense of belonging.

HISTORY OF STAR

The Rotary Club of El Paso started this program in July 1976 and it has been very evident that the Club has a better informed membership and that 'retention' of members has improved. The Leaders of the club today have all come from the **STAR** program. New members who will likely become future leaders in the club, can generally be identified in their first year in Rotary. Over 85% of the Rotarians in the Rotary Club of El Paso are graduates of this program and they are proud to have become Rotarians through the **STAR** committee.

THE SPUR BOOKLET, which is used for the curriculum for each meeting, is published by **District 5520** *every three years after every Council on Legislation, except where there are so few changes that it would not warrant a new printing expense. The Spur Booklet is available to all clubs in the District and has been shared along with the STAR information throughout the Rotary world and adopted by many, including Mexico.* **District 4110, our sister District,** *received approval to translate both programs into Spanish for their members. One Rotary District, using the SPUR Booklet calls their program RICE (Rotary Information Continu-*

ing Education). West El Paso Rotary calls their program GEAR (Getting Educated About Rotary).

*The authors of these programs are **Past District Governor Vince Ward of the Rotary Club of El Paso and Past President of the Club, Jim Stewart.** They have passed on since, but both Vince and Jim were always willing to assist any club or district interested in these programs.*

Irving J. "Sonny" Brown, Past RI Vice President and Trustee of the Rotary Foundation of Rotary International will be pleased to assist in carrying forward this program and is willing to provide additional information as may be requested.

Contact Sonny at:

200 Bartlett Dr. # 105
El Paso, Texas 79912
Phone-915-584-5511
FAX -915-584-6315
sonny@sonnybrown.com

APPENDIX F

Additional Resources

Many RI publications and videos directed toward membership development are listed below. All items may be ordered from the Publications Order Services Section in the USA (telephone: 847-866-4600; fax: 847-866-3276) or the RI international offices. For language availability, please consult the *RI Catalog* (019) or the online catalog.

Look under Membership on Rotary's Web page (www.rotary.org) for information for prospective and new members and organizing new clubs, plus current global membership statistics, membership success ideas submitted by clubs and districts worldwide, questionnaires for use by your club, and a wealth of other membership ideas and resources for clubs and districts.

E-LEARNING CENTER

The E-Learning Center is a webpage that contains learning modules for new member orientation and club officer reference and training. These modules are displayed in Microsoft PowerPoint and Adobe PDF format that can be viewed or saved to your hard drive.

The E-Learning Center can be reached by selecting the Training link from the menu bar on the Rotary website. From Training, select E-Learning Center from the left sidebar menu options. The page can also be reached by going directly to:

http://www.rotary.org/training/elearning/index.html

Title	Description	Catalog Number	Available on the Web
ABCs of Rotary, The	A compact guide through Rotary's history, customs, and traditions originating from a compilation of short articles first written by past RI President Cliff Dochterman.	363	No
Demographic Survey Template	A tool to help clubs review their membership data. This Microsoft Access download contains a questionnaire and automatically tabulates information entered by club members.		Yes - Web Only
History of Rotary	A new seven-minute video that summarizes the history of Rotary since its founding in 1905.	921	No
How to Propose a New Member	Brochure includes the basic procedure for election of a new member. (Includes one copy of the Membership Proposal Form.)	254	Yes
Membership Development Resource Guide	A booklet that outlines basic procedures for building club membership through retention and recruitment. Offers ideas and resources for effective club membership development strategies.	417	No
Membership Growth and Development	A booklet featuring information on a variety of membership development ideas, tools, and suggestions for use by clubs.	916	No
Membership Identification Card	Supplied to every Rotarian by the club secretary to verify membership. Vendor contact information available on the Membership area of the RI web site.		
New Member Orientation	Guidelines for conducting effective orientation for new members	414	No

Organizing New Clubs: A Guide for District Governors and Special Representatives	This publication outlines the procedures for the creation of a new club. Includes required forms and suggestions for ensuring the effectiveness and longevity of the new club.	808	Forms Only
Presidential Citation Brochure	Leaflet that outlines the Presidential Citation Program.	9001A	Yes
Presidential Citation Certification Form		9001B	Yes
RI Catalog	A list of RI publications, audiovisual tools, books and periodicals, forms, and supplies. Web version available at www.rotary.org. New print edition available each June.	019	Yes
RI Membership Development and Extension Award	Brochure outlining this annual certificate award program for clubs and districts.	901	Yes
RI Print PSAs	Three images on a compact disc highlighting the faces of Rotary and the importance of investing in one's community with the tag line, "A global network of community volunteers."	345	
Rotary Basics	An excellent orientation tool as well as a refresher course on Rotary International and Rotary Foundation information.	595	No
Rotary: Connecting Lives, Affecting Lives (Print PSAs)	Images of Rotarians engaged in polio immunizations, an Australian Rotarian effort to help families displaced by fires, and a Canadian Rotarian mobile clinic serving the homeless. Useful for publications, stationery, and billboards. (EN only)	015	No

Rotary: Connecting Lives, Affecting Lives (Television PSAs)	One 90-second and three 30- and 60-second PSAs featuring Rotary's polio eradication effort, an Australian Rotary program to help families who lost homes to bush fires, and a Rotary-sponsored mobile clinic in Canada. (EN only)	179	No
Rotary Fact Pack	A package of fact sheets on various aspects of Rotary, updated quarterly. Regional fact packs are also available upon request.	267	Yes
Rotary Foundation Annual Report	Illustrated report on The Rotary Foundation's programs and audited finances.	187B	Yes
Rotary Foundation Print PSAs	Six images loaded on a compact disc portraying the work of The Rotary Foundation with the tag line, "Rotarians Make A Difference."	335	No
Rotary Gives People an Opportunity to Help	Two 30- and 60-second television PSAs featuring Rotary projects to help street children in Brazil and a baseball league for disabled children in the USA. Intended to raise awareness of Rotary, these membership development PSAs target a North American audience. (EN only)	341	No
Rotary International Annual Report	Illustrated highlights of the Rotary year, plus audited finances.	187A	Yes
Rotary in Your Community	A 30-minute video providing a comprehensive overview of Rotary club service and members. Excellent for use as prepackaged programming for local cable access stations.	332	No
Rotary Makes a Difference	Six 30-second television spots highlight the work of The Rotary Foundation: "Preserving Planet Earth," "Promoting Peace," "Helping Children," "Increasing Education," "Working to Eradicate Polio," and "Feeding the Hungry." Each spot ends, "Rotary Makes A Difference."	338	No

Rotary News Basket	A weekly four-page report of Rotary news and short features. (annual subscription)	546	Yes
Rotary World	Eight-page, tabloid-size newspaper (yearly subscription). Available via the Circulation Department at RI World Headquarters (telephone: 847-866-3171; e-mail: data@rotaryintl.org.	050	Yes
Rotary: Your Choice for Change	Designed specifically for North Americans, this new video targets prospective Rotarians within the 35-45 year age range by highlighting dynamic clubs and their community service projects.	919	No
Service Above Self	A 30-second television PSA showing Rotarians' good work around the globe.	070	No
Take a Look at Rotary	Designed specifically for prospective Rotarians in North America, the video provides an informative introduction to the many aspects of club membership.	867	No
This is Rotary	A video that provides a comprehensive overview of Rotary, its goals and service programs, the Avenues of Service, and the diverse service projects sponsored by Rotary clubs and The Rotary Foundation. (DVD - 449v - EN only)	449 449v	No No
This is Rotary	Brochure providing an overview of Rotary for prospective Rotarians and the public.	001	Yes
What's Rotary	Handy, wallet-size card answering frequently asked questions about the organization and scope of Rotary. Popular as a handout to non-Rotarians.	419	No

The Rotary Foundation and the Public Relations Division of RI produce additional materials that may be used for recruitment and member education. Please consult the *RI Catalog* (019) for more resources.

Make *Frank Talk* work for your club and district

  Tens of thousands of Rotarians the world over have used *Frank Talk* to tell the story of Rotary—and help bring in new members.

Now you can use *Frank Talk II* to show your members how to do their part to energize their club and make members more active and involved—and keep wavering members from leaving!